THE WHOLESOME *yum*®

EASY KETO
CARBOHOLICS' *cookbook*

MAYA KRAMPF
USA TODAY Best-Selling Author

100 LOW CARB
COMFORT FOOD RECIPES.

—

10 INGREDIENTS
OR LESS.

CONTENTS

GETTING STARTED

I've been living a low carb lifestyle for over a decade, and it has made an immeasurable difference in my life. My struggles with low energy, anxiety, and yo-yo eating are gone. Truth be told, I'm not perfect at it—I have my setbacks just like most people—but I try to be as consistent as I can. My mantra with food, "done is better than perfect," is the same one that has spilled over into so many other life areas, even if the perfectionist in me from years ago would have never believed it.

When people hear about how long I've been eating low carb or keto, the most common responses are disbelief or criticism—disbelief that it's really possible to uphold for this long, or criticism of me missing out on "essential carbs." The truth is, there is no such thing. Even for processes that require glucose, low carb vegetables provide a decent amount, and the body is able to extract the rest from the protein we eat via gluconeogenesis. Through all my research on nutrition over the years, I've come to realize that focusing on nutrient density and eating whole foods are far more important.

That doesn't make it any easier, though, does it? Essential or not, we still *miss* those carbs. A lot. Many people embarking on a keto journey for the first time are skeptical about sustaining it, because the idea of giving up carbs for the long term is so daunting.

That is why, through the many years that I have been doing this, there is one thing that has helped me stick to this way of eating: the ability to make **low carb versions of my favorite carb-filled foods**. I really struggled until I was able to figure this out. It does *not* mean that these foods are all that I eat, or all that you *should* eat, but it does make this lifestyle sustainable—and delicious.

It turns out, these types of foods are favorites among my readers, too. The most popular recipes from my first book, *The Easy Keto Cookbook*, were the comfort foods and carb replacements, such as bread, chili, pizza, and desserts.

That's why I was so excited to write ***The Easy Keto Carboholics' Cookbook***, dedicated to all the carboholics out there that struggle with giving up carbs, just like I did. This book is filled with recipes to replace your favorite comfort foods, including bread, pasta, rice, potatoes, pizza, desserts, and more. And just like the ones on my website and in my first book, each recipe has ten ingredients or less (not including salt and pepper), because I'm all about keeping things simple and easy.

If you're excited about the benefits of a low carb lifestyle, but the idea of giving up carbs is giving you a hard time, you don't have to worry anymore. **You got this!**

MAKE KETO EASIER WITH THE WHOLESOME YUM APP

Use my app to track your macros (including thousands of foods and recipes), plan your meals (with custom meal plans), get automatic grocery lists, AND keep all the recipes from this book conveniently on your phone!

DOWNLOAD IT AT www.wholesomeyum.com/get-the-app OR scan the QR code on any recipe page in this book!

KETO FLOURS & BAKING INGREDIENTS

Almost all baked goods can be made keto friendly — it's just less straightforward than using traditional white flour and sugar. Instead of using a single flour for all applications, we use a variety of them to achieve the right texture in low carb baking: almond and coconut flours, psyllium husk powder, flaxseed meal, xanthan gum, protein powder, and sometimes even cheese.

Often, we have to combine multiple ingredients to get the result we want. If you are accustomed to white flour, which can be used as a single ingredient in many different ways, this may be an adjustment. With keto ingredients, the combination that works best depends largely on the desired texture: crispy or soft, airy or dense, cake-like or chewy, and so on. Achieving the result you want gets easier with practice, though, and this book is a great jumping off point to familiarize yourself with the essential keto baking staples.

First, I want to introduce you to each of these common low carb baking ingredients and how to measure them, so that you can better understand how they function, their purpose, and the best ways to use them.

HOW TO MEASURE DRY INGREDIENTS

Measure low carb flours the same way you would measure regular white flour:

- Scoop with your measuring cup or spoon. Do not pack the flour into the measuring cup!
- Holding the measuring cup or spoon over the opened bag, level the top with a knife, letting any excess fall back into the bag.

ALMOND FLOUR

- **What it is:** Blanched almond flour is simply almonds that have had their skins removed and have been ground into a flour.
- **What it does:** While it does not act exactly like white flour, almond flour makes the easiest white flour replacement in recipes, both sweet and savory. You can usually replace white flour with almond flour cup for cup, and then add small amounts of other ingredients if you need a chewy texture or a dough that holds together.
- **What it won't do:** Almond flour will not get very crispy as a breading (especially if baked), create chewy baked goods on its own, or do a good job with light, airy items. Crispy breading requires adding something that does crisp up, such as whey protein powder or crushed pork rinds. Chewy baked goods are possible with the addition of psyllium husk powder, flaxseed meal, xanthan gum, or cheese if making fathead dough, which uses a combination of melted mozzarella, cream cheese, eggs, and a keto friendly flour (see page 15). Airy baked goods are challenging with keto ingredients in general, but combining almond flour with protein powder, whipped egg whites, or a lot more baking powder than you may be used to can help, depending on the application.
- **What to look for:** Even the finest almond flour is coarser than white flour, but you can get reasonably similar results with super fine blanched almond flour. Blanching removes the skins, which can cause baked goods to be grainy. Unblanched almond flour is often called almond meal and almost always produces inferior results in recipes. In addition, the grinding process varies among

brands, so some are coarser than others, even if they are labeled blanched and super fine.

- **Substitutions:** While there is no other flour that behaves exactly like almond flour, the closest nut-free substitution would be sunflower seed meal. Just be aware that it's not as fine as blanched almond flour, so your baked goods may be grainier. It also has a tendency to turn baked goods green because of the way it reacts with baking powder, but these are still safe to eat. Other nut flours, such as macadamia nut flour or hazelnut flour, can be used instead of almond flour for naturally denser items, such as pie crusts or cookies.

COCONUT FLOUR

- **What it is:** Coconut flour, a natural byproduct of coconut milk production, is made from dried coconut meat that is very finely ground.
- **What it does:** People commonly turn to coconut flour because they have a nut allergy or notice that it's much less expensive than almond flour; however, it is probably the most challenging flour to work with. Because it absorbs so much moisture, and continues to do so as it sits in a batter or dough, coconut flour can be very drying for baked goods. To compensate, special recipes developed specifically for coconut flour must be used. You can find some included in this book. Coconut flour can sometimes help create the right consistency in a batter or dough that would otherwise be too wet.
- **What it won't do:** Like almond flour, coconut flour will not get crispy as a breading. In fact, it should almost never be used for breading, as it's too fine, but it

ABOUT WHOLESOME YUM FLOURS

I've sourced the highest quality ingredients for the keto baking staples I use most often, because I wanted consistent quality I can count on in my recipes. For example, even almond flour brands labeled "super fine" can vary in their consistency, which is why I created **Wholesome Yum Super Fine Blanched Almond Flour**—the finest grind you'll find anywhere.

Wholesome Yum flours currently include:

- **Super Fine Blanched Almond Flour:** www.wholesomeyumfoods.com/shop/flours/almond-flour
- **Organic Coconut Flour:** www.wholesomeyumfoods.com/shop/flours/coconut-flour
- **Psyllium Husk Powder:** www.wholesomeyumfoods.com/shop/flours/psyllium-husk-powder
- **More coming soon!**

When you shop these ingredients, you not only get the highest quality, you also help support my books as well.

works great for dredging. Aside from drying out easily, coconut flour baked goods also tend to be dense and crumbly, but they can be improved with the same additions that almond flour benefits from: psyllium husk powder, flaxseed meal, xanthan gum, or cheese if making fathead dough. Avoid coconut flour altogether for any airy baked goods, unless using very small amounts, as they will not get enough lift.

- **What to look for:** If you measure and weigh different brands of coconut flour, you'll notice that the weight of a cup can vary fairly significantly and this, in turn, affects how much moisture will be absorbed in your recipes. For this reason, use the brand that was used to develop the recipe, if possible (all my recipes use Wholesome Yum Coconut Flour), or measure by weight when those measurements are available.

- **Substitutions:** Do not replace any other flour (low carb or not) with coconut flour in a recipe, as this almost never works. Almond flour often can be replaced with coconut flour in a recipe by using just a quarter of the flour amount and adding an extra egg, but this rule of thumb is not guaranteed and will depend on the specific recipe.

WHEY PROTEIN POWDER

- **What it is:** Whey protein powder is protein from whey, a byproduct of cheesemaking, that has been dried and powdered.
- **What it does:** Adding protein powder to other keto flours in baked goods is a great way to mimic the structural qualities of gluten (also a protein). It also helps to lift doughs and batters, making them lighter than those using almond or coconut flour alone. For breading applications, whey protein powder crisps up nicely when fried, particularly when mixed with almond flour. Of course, it adds a boost of protein to your foods as well.
- **What it won't do:** While protein powder does help with structure, it will not make doughs stretchy like gluten would. For that, you'd need a Fathead Dough with mozzarella (page 15), psyllium husk powder, or xanthan gum.

- **What to look for:** Protein powders are notorious for having added fillers and even sugars, so it's important to look for one without any additional ingredients. Whey protein powder comes in two main forms, whey protein isolate and whey protein concentrate. Both work in recipes, but the former is more pure, significantly lower in carbs, and more expensive. Ideally, look for a brand of whey protein isolate that has zero carbs.
- **Substitutions:** Egg white protein powder usually makes a good substitute for whey protein powder in baking, but it is not recommended in breading, where the results come out chewy. Collagen protein powder is also fine to use when the purpose is simply to provide protein content, but it does not have the same benefit of improving the texture of your baked goods. Results with other types of protein powder can be hit or miss, depending on the recipe, and some substitutes are also higher in carbs.

XANTHAN GUM

- **What it is:** Xanthan gum is a food additive produced by fermentation.
- **What it does:** Xanthan gum is used in baking to provide structure (as in cakes or muffins), pliability (as in tortillas), and/or chewiness (as in bread or cookies). Gluten is responsible for these qualities in baked goods made with white flour, but for keto items using low carb flours, xanthan gum is often needed to make up for these missing characteristics. Xanthan gum can also act as an emulsifier or thickening agent in sauces, soups, etc.
- **What it won't do:** Xanthan gum is intended for use in very small amounts and is not a

bulking agent. It can result in a slimy texture if too much is used.

- **What to look for:** Most brands of xanthan gum will function the same way in recipes, but look for non-GMO if possible.
- **Substitutions:** In baking, the easiest replacements for xanthan gum are glucomannan (also known as konjac powder; use 1 to 1½ times the amount), locust bean gum (use double the amount), or guar gum (use 1½ times the amount). Sometimes unflavored gelatin powder can be used as well, but you'd usually need 5 to 10 times the amount. If structure or thickness is not super critical in the food you are making, such as in cookies, you can omit xanthan gum, knowing that the end result will simply be less chewy. For applications where gum is intended as a thickener, such as in soups or sauces, you can also thicken with other ingredients instead, such as cream cheese or pureed vegetables.

PSYLLIUM HUSK POWDER

- **What it is:** Psyllium husk powder is a ground form of psyllium husks, the outer coating of the seeds of the psyllium plant. It's a great natural source of soluble fiber, and prebiotic.
- **What it does:** Psyllium husk powder functions as a thickener, binding agent, and texture enhancer, all in one. Add small amounts of powder (most commonly 2 to 6 tablespoons, depending on the recipe) to any baking recipe in which a chewy texture is desired, such as bread or pizza crust. Because psyllium husk powder absorbs a lot of moisture, additional water or other liquid will be needed.
- **What it won't do:** Psyllium husk powder can create an undesirable, slimy, or even gritty

texture in baked goods if too much of it is used, so it's best to stick to tested recipes when possible. If you want to experiment on your own, start with just a couple of tablespoons, or no more than one quarter of the dry ingredient volume, and remember to add extra liquid. While psyllium husk powder definitely acts as a thickener (it absorbs a lot of moisture), it is not recommended for thickening sauces, soups, or stews because the resulting texture will not be smooth.

- **What to look for:** Psyllium husk powder ranges in purity level (typically 95% to 99%), though this information is often not adequately labeled. Less pure powders will have slightly higher carb counts, while the highest grades (such as Wholesome Yum Psyllium Husk Powder) will have zero net carbs.
- **Substitutions:** Flaxseed meal often makes a 1:1 substitute for psyllium husk powder in baking, though the latter tends to create a chewier result. Ground chia seeds sometimes work as a replacement as well.

FLAXSEED MEAL

- **What it is:** Flaxseed meal is simply ground flaxseeds, which are a great source of fiber and omega-3 fatty acids.
- **What it does:** Similar to psyllium husk powder, flaxseed meal can be a great thickener, binding agent, and texture enhancer for chewier baked goods. It can also be used to create an egg replacement (often called a "flax egg") in baking, by mixing one part flaxseed meal with three parts water and letting the mixture sit for 15 minutes.
- **What it won't do:** Flaxseed meal does help with chewiness and structure, but generally

to a lesser extent than psyllium husk powder. Flax eggs make a decent substitute for eggs in baked goods but are less sturdy than real eggs. They work best where structure and flexibility are less important—think muffins or cakes rather than pliable flatbreads.

- **What to look for:** I always recommend golden flaxseed meal over the regular brown kind because it has a more neutral flavor.
- **Substitutions:** Psyllium husk powder or ground chia seeds can usually replace flaxseed meal in most baking applications, just like the reverse is true.

LUPIN FLOUR

- **What it is:** Lupin flour is a low carb, high fiber flour made from lupin beans, which are a part of the legume family (like peanuts), and can be found online.
- **What it does:** Unlike other keto friendly flours, lupin flour is high in protein, and that protein can mimic the properties of gluten, albeit to a lesser extent. This makes it an ideal candidate for making pasta (see 3-Ingredient Egg Noodles on page 114), but it can also work in place of almond flour for muffins, breads, etc. Like almond flour, lupin flour can be combined with psyllium husk powder, whey protein powder, xanthan gum, or, for fathead dough, mozzarella.
- **What it won't do:** Plain lupin flour can taste a little bitter, but this is not usually noticeable once you mix it with other ingredients for baking. Still, you may detect an earthy taste if a large amount of lupin flour is used in a recipe.
- **What to look for:** Lupin flour can be difficult to find in stores, but any brand you find online will work fine.

- **Substitutions:** Almond flour is the closest substitute for lupin flour, but it is higher in fat and lower in protein, so the results are a bit different.

MOZZARELLA

- **What it is:** Mozzarella is a semi-soft cheese made from cow's milk.
- **What it does:** Mozzarella is used in baked goods when making fathead dough (see page 15 for more details), which has a chewy, bready texture remarkably similar to traditional pizza crust.
- **What it won't do:** Dough made with cheese is designed for chewy baked goods, such as pizza crusts, calzones, or bagels, so don't use it when you want a crumb texture. Mozzarella is primarily savory or neutral, but mildly sweet versions are possible by adding up to a few tablespoons of sweetener. Depending on your kitchen temperature, mozzarella dough can be too sticky to work with immediately, but it becomes workable after chilling in the refrigerator. Too much sweetener, however, will makes this type of dough too sticky to work with, even after chilling.
- **What to look for:** To use mozzarella for baking, you'll want low-moisture mozzarella, which is usually part-skim. Avoid fresh mozzarella (the snow white kind that comes as a ball) as this will have too much water content.
- **Substitutions:** Semi-soft and semi-hard cheeses, such as Cheddar or Jack, can be used in place of mozzarella for fathead dough, but the flavor will be more cheesy and less neutral.

EGGS

- **What it is:** Eggs are a staple on the keto diet in general, and are also commonly used in keto baking in the same ways as in traditional baking.
- **What it does:** Eggs provide structure, leavening, richness, color, and flavor in baked goods. The structure and leavening aspects are particularly important in low carb baking, which uses flours that lack structure and do not rise as well as wheat flour.
- **What it won't do:** While eggs do a great job of providing structure, they are not enough on their own to replace the gluten that white flour has. If you want a chewy texture or low carb baked goods that hold together as well as their regular counterparts, you will need to add other ingredients, such as xanthan gum, psyllium husk powder, or flaxseed meal.
- **What to look for:** Most recipes will use large eggs or specify the size they call for. Wholesome Yum recipes always use large eggs. I prefer to buy organic, cage-free eggs for the best nutritional value, but any kind will work from a recipe standpoint.
- **Substitutions:** In baked goods, you can often replace eggs with flax eggs by mixing 1 part flaxseed meal with 3 parts water and letting the mixture sit for 15 minutes. Flax eggs, however, will provide less structure than real eggs.

BAKING POWDER

- **What it is:** Baking powder is a leavening agent, composed of baking soda, cream of tartar, and sometimes cornstarch. Cornstarch is not keto friendly on its own, but baking powder is fine to use since it includes only a small amount of it.
- **What it does:** Baking powder makes your baked goods rise and prevents them from being too dense. The critical components of baking powder are baking soda (a base) and cream of tartar (an acid); when exposed to liquid, they react to create bubbles. Most baking powders are double-acting, meaning they react once when mixed with liquid and again when heated during baking.
- **What it won't do:** Baking powder will not fully make up for the fact that low carb flours tend to produce denser baked goods than their white flour counterparts, but it can help. Often, 1½ to 2 times more baking powder than usual is needed to compensate for this tendency.
- **What to look for:** For best results, look for an aluminum-free baking powder. I also prefer brands that are non-GMO.
- **Substitutions:** If you prefer to avoid the cornstarch present in commercial baking powders, you can make your own by mixing 2 parts cream of tartar with 1 part baking soda. Do not substitute baking soda for baking powder in recipes, as this will result in a metallic, soapy taste and will not have the desired leavening effect.

KETO SWEETENERS

I talked a lot about sweeteners in my first book, *The Wholesome Yum Easy Keto Cookbook*, but I'd be remiss if I didn't mention sugar replacements in a book about replacing carbs. In addition, there are some new sweeteners I have started using since the first book was written, so this guide offers a more current perspective.

MONK FRUIT

Monk fruit, also known as luo han guo, is a small Asian melon that has been used in Chinese medicine for centuries. Monk fruit extract is derived by crushing the fruit, then drying the juice into a concentrated powder that has no calories, carbs, or sugar.

Monk fruit extract is extremely sweet—150 to 400 times sweeter than sugar—because of an antioxidant in the fruit called mogroside V. Because their sweetness is so concentrated, monk fruit sweeteners deemed as sugar replacements are actually blends of monk fruit extract and a bulking agent. Most brands use erythritol (see below) as the bulking agent, which is a decent choice.

However, Besti Monk Fruit Sweetener (also sometimes called Besti Monk Fruit Allulose Blend, which is used throughout this book) includes allulose as its bulking agent instead, because allulose tastes and acts much more like sugar and does not crystallize, generate a minty "cooling" aftertaste, resist dissolving, or cause stomach upset in most people—all issues common to erythritol. The combination of monk fruit and allulose ensures that, unlike most other monk fruit sweeteners, Besti measures cup for cup like sugar.

In addition, different brands of monk fruit extract come with different levels of mogroside V, which affects how sweet they are and whether they have any aftertaste. The monk fruit extract in Besti sweeteners is the highest grade, with 50% mogroside V and no aftertaste.

ALLULOSE

Allulose is a natural sugar that we can't metabolize, which means it tastes and acts like sugar without spiking our blood sugar. Found in fruit, maple syrup, and other plants, it's 70% as sweet as sugar.

The name "allulose" sounds like glucose, fructose, lactose, and other sugar names, because it's in the same family. This is what makes it so incredibly similar to sugar in both taste and function in recipes. Unlike other sugars, though, we can't process allulose, which means it has nearly zero calories and zero net carbs.

Being part of the sugar family gives allulose distinct advantages over other low carb sweeteners. Unlike others, it dissolves and caramelizes like sugar would. It's also a natural preservative and locks in moisture, resulting in soft baked goods that last a little longer. These same advantages are present with Besti Monk Fruit Allulose Blend, since allulose is a big part of it. The additional benefits of allulose are mentioned in the section above, where I discuss why I use allulose as a bulking agent in Besti.

ERYTHRITOL

Erythritol is part of the family of sugar alcohols, which are found in nature, but has some unique properties compared to others, such as sorbitol or maltitol. Erythritol is the only sweetener in this family that has a glycemic index of zero and is easier to digest than others, though still more prone to causing stomach upset when compared to allulose.

Like allulose, erythritol has zero calories, zero net carbs, and 70% the sweetness of sugar. Although you can use pure erythritol, it's commonly blended with high-intensity sweeteners, like monk fruit or stevia, since it's less sweet than sugar on its own. In fact, most brands labeled "monk fruit" or "stevia" are actually almost all erythritol, with small amounts of monk fruit or stevia added to achieve the desired sweetness level.

Erythritol was my go-to keto sweetener for years, before Besti existed and allulose was widely available, and it's still a solid choice. That being said, it's not my favorite anymore because the performance of Besti (or even just plain allulose) is just so much closer to that of real sugar. I like not having to struggle with crystallization, cooling aftertastes, or sweeteners that do not dissolve.

STEVIA

Like monk fruit, stevia is a very concentrated natural sweetener, up to 150 times as sweet as sugar, derived from the stevia rebaudiana plant. Stevia leaves have been used in some cultures for more than one thousand years. I have never been a fan of stevia because it has a noticeable bitter aftertaste.

Pure stevia comes as a concentrated powder and as a liquid, but both are difficult to use in recipes because they lack the volume that sugar would have and the intense sweetness makes it easy to use too much. Many brands of stevia, like brands of monk fruit, blend stevia with erythritol or another filler to allow for a cup-for-cup measurement like sugar. Unfortunately, adding erythritol leads to the same problems mentioned in the section above, and brands without erythritol typically use hidden sugars, such as maltodextrin, as their bulking agents.

If you do decide to consider stevia sweeteners and do not mind the aftertaste, be aware that stevia is part of the ragweed family, so you'll want to avoid it if you have an allergy to ragweed. You may also want to experiment with different brands, as some people find that some are more bitter than others.

XYLITOL

Xylitol is a sugar alcohol, in the same family as erythritol. Unlike erythritol, though, xylitol is not zero calorie (it has about two-thirds the calories of sugar), and there is some controversy about whether it's really zero net carb. The glycemic index of xylitol is 7, compared to 0 for erythritol and 65 for table sugar.

The advantage of xylitol over erythritol is that it already measures cup for cup like sugar and dissolves better. Unfortunately, its significant drawbacks include common stomach upset and the fact that it is lethal to dogs. These factors, combined with the higher glycemic index, make it a less ideal choice.

CONSIDERATIONS WHEN USING KETO SWEETENERS

When making the recipes in this book, I highly recommend using the Besti sweeteners called for, as results can be different with other sugar substitutes. If you experiment with different sweeteners, consider these factors:

- **Level of sweetness:** If you are swapping sweeteners, check if they have the same sweetness level. Pure erythritol and pure allulose are 70% as sweet as sugar, pure monk fruit or stevia can be hundreds of times sweeter than sugar, and many other

ABOUT BESTI SWEETENERS

The recipes in this book exclusively use Besti Monk Fruit Allulose Blends as sweeteners, including crystallized, powdered, and brown versions.

- Sweet like sugar—replaces sugar cup for cup
- Tastes like sugar, with no aftertaste
- Bakes like sugar and helps baked goods stay moist
- Dissolves like sugar, unlike most sweeteners
- Browns and caramelizes like sugar, unlike most sweeteners
- Keto friendly
- 100% natural
- Non-GMO
- Will not crystallize
- Does not cause stomach upset

Order Besti sweeteners and other Wholesome Yum keto food products at www.wholesomeyumfoods.com. When you shop for these ingredients, you not only get the highest quality, you also help support my books as well.

1:1 sugar replacements (such as Besti) have the same sweetness as sugar, making them the easiest to use. You may need to adjust the amount if the sweetness level of your chosen sweetener is different from what is called for, but watch for issues with the wet vs. dry ingredient ratio (see below).

- **Texture:** Just as regular sugar comes in granulated, powdered, and brown forms, so do sugar alternatives. Each of these will behave in a distinct way, so be sure to use the form called for in recipes. When experimenting on your own, use granulated for the best texture in general baking, powdered for smooth consistencies (such as frosting, custard, sauce, dressing, or cheesecake filling), and brown when you want the flavor and moisture of brown sugar. If you only have granulated sweetener and a recipe calls for powdered, you can powder it at home using a coffee grinder or powerful food processor.
- **Wet vs. dry ratio:** Sugar substitutes do more in recipes than simply provide sweetness: They can also affect moisture and provide bulk. This is why it's not a good idea to replace a liquid sweetener with a granulated one, or a cup-for-cup granulated sweetener with a very concentrated powder. You will throw off the consistency of your batter if the difference in your sweetener form or volume is too drastic.
- **Browning:** Most low carb sugar substitutes will not brown or caramelize like sugar does. In fact, the only ones that do are pure allulose and allulose-based sweeteners, such as Besti.
- **Dissolving:** Most sugar-free granulated sweeteners do not dissolve well, even when heated. Pure allulose and allulose-based sweeteners, such as Besti, will dissolve the same way as sugar would. If you don't have one of these, be sure the sweetener you do use is at least powdered, which will make it more likely to dissolve.
- **Aftertaste:** Pure stevia and pure monk fruit extract tend to have a bitter aftertaste, while erythritol (or any brand that uses it as a bulking agent) can have a "cooling effect." Allulose-based sweeteners, including Besti, have no aftertaste.

WHAT TO AVOID

Occasionally, people ask me about other sweeteners and whether they are okay to eat on keto. For the most part, I only recommend the ones listed above, but just for clarity, here are the three main categories to avoid:

- **Sugar:** All types of sugar—white table sugar, date sugar, coconut sugar, powdered sugar, etc. If it has sugar in the name, skip it. In addition, watch for hidden names for sugar, including maltodextrin and anything ending with "ose" (dextrose, lactose, glucose, sucrose, fructose, etc.). Allulose is the only exception to this rule, as explained on page 11.

- **Syrups:** Any syrup that is not sugar-free will not be keto friendly. This includes maple syrup, agave, corn syrup, and honey. Although some of these sweeteners are natural and touted as healthy, they will still spike your blood sugar and kick you out of ketosis, the same way that sugar would. (If you want to learn more about ketosis, read about it in my first book, *The Wholesome Yum Easy Keto Cookbook*, or on my website at **www.wholesomeyum.com**.)

- **Artificial sweeteners:** These include sucralose, aspartame, and saccharin, among others. Unlike the natural sweeteners that I recommend above, artificial sweeteners do not exist in nature. Even in the short time they have been around, there have been conflicting studies about whether the common artificial sweeteners are safe. Besides, artificial sweeteners often have an artificial aftertaste and don't usually measure the same way as sugar. With several delicious, natural options available, there's no reason to turn to artificial ones.

FATHEAD DOUGH

Fathead dough is a keto friendly dough made from mozzarella cheese, cream cheese, eggs, and a low carb flour, typically almond or coconut. The combination of melted cheeses with a low carb flour creates a dough that is stretchy and flexible when raw and remarkably similar to that of white flour goods when baked.

This dough was originally created as a recipe for pizza crust—and the texture is incredibly close to regular pizza crust (see page 92 for a deep-dish version). However, you can also use it for numerous other baked goods, like Soft Pretzels (page 34), 3-Ingredient Egg Noodles (page 114), and Sticky Monkey Bread (page 198), as well as twists on classic pizza, like White Pizza Pockets (page 101) and Pepperoni Pizza Rolls (page 102).

> My first book, **The Wholesome Yum Easy Keto Cookbook**, has a more in-depth guide and pictures illustrating how to work with fathead dough, including additional tips and variations, alternate methods for forming the dough, storage and freezing instructions, and more. Pick up a copy at **www.wholesomeyum.com/cookbook**.

MOST IMPORTANT TIPS

- **Use a food processor, if possible.** A food processor is the fastest, easiest, and most effective way to make fathead dough, but if you don't have one, you can mix the dough by hand. You'll want to whisk the egg separately before mixing it with the flour in step 1 and use your hands to knead the cheese into the flour mixture in step 3.
- **Mix well.** The dough should be uniform and free of streaks of flour or cheese. If the

HOW TO MAKE FATHEAD DOUGH

You can make fathead dough with almond flour or coconut flour. The ingredient amounts are different, but the process is the same.

ALMOND FLOUR VERSION

¾ cup (3 ounces) super fine blanched almond flour

1 large egg

1½ cups (6 ounces) shredded mozzarella cheese

2 tablespoons (1 ounce) cream cheese, cut into cubes

COCONUT FLOUR VERSION

⅓ cup (1⅓ ounces) coconut flour

2 large eggs

1½ cups (6 ounces) shredded mozzarella cheese

2 tablespoons (1 ounce) cream cheese, cut into cubes

INSTRUCTIONS

1. In a food processor, process the almond or coconut flour and egg(s), until smooth.

2. In a large bowl, microwave the mozzarella and cream cheese for about 90 seconds, or heat in a double boiler on the stove, stirring halfway through, until smooth.

3. Add the cheese to the food processor, positioning the cheese so that the blades are sticking into it, and process until a dough forms. Pulse or scrape the sides as necessary.

cheese solidifies too much and no longer wants to mix in (this is more common when making the dough by hand), you can microwave the dough for about 30 seconds to soften it and help it come together.

- **Chill if necessary.** This dough can be sticky when it's first made, depending on your kitchen temperature. If it's too sticky to work with immediately, or especially if you'll be forming shapes with it, it's best to chill it first. Do your best to form the dough into a ball, then cover and refrigerate it for about 30 minutes, until it's cool to the touch (but not frigid cold) and less sticky.

- **Use oiled hands and/or parchment paper.** Fathead dough is easiest to roll out between two sheets of lightly oiled parchment paper. If you need to form shapes with it or fold it with your hands, put a bit of oil on your hands first.

- **Avoid too much sweetener.** If you are making this dough for a sweet recipe, limit the sweetener to only a few tablespoons. Otherwise, the dough can become too sticky, even after chilling.

RICE SUBSTITUTES

The primary substitute for rice when following a low carb lifestyle is cauliflower rice, which is simply cauliflower cut into rice shapes. It has a neutral flavor that makes it perfect for taking on the flavors of any dish, just as white rice would. As a bonus, it's also very easy to make (much quicker than rice!) and is a healthy way to get your veggies.

Cauliflower rice is a staple for many keto followers and is used throughout this book, so familiarize yourself with it! Then, branch out to variations on the basic, like Cilantro Lime Cauliflower Rice (page 69) and Dirty Cauliflower Rice (page 73), and try it as a component in recipes, like Cauliflower Wild Rice Soup (page 55) and Mexican Beef & Rice Stuffed Peppers (page 143).

WAYS TO MAKE CAULIFLOWER RICE

You can make cauliflower rice yourself from a head of cauliflower, or you can buy it. Here are all the different methods:

- **Food processor method:** For longer "rice grains," feed cauliflower florets into a food processor fitted with a grater attachment, while the food processor is running. For smaller bits (similar to couscous), place the florets into a food processor fitted with an S blade and pulse intermittently until you achieve the desired consistency.
- **Box grater method:** Grate cauliflower florets against the sides of the box grater with medium or large holes to get pieces about the size of rice.

- **Knife method:** Using a knife is not recommended, but if you don't have a food processor or box grater, you can essentially mince your cauliflower florets until the pieces are super fine.
- **Buy cauliflower rice:** This is available fresh or frozen at the grocery store. Fresh goes bad very quickly, but frozen will keep for several months.

HOW TO COOK CAULIFLOWER RICE

SERVING SIZE 1 cup | **SERVES 4**

INGREDIENTS

1 medium head cauliflower, or 4 cups riced cauliflower, fresh or frozen

½ teaspoon sea salt, or to taste

⅛ teaspoon black pepper, or to taste

2 tablespoons olive oil

INSTRUCTIONS

1. Make cauliflower rice using a box grater or food processor. (Skip if you have pre-made or frozen cauliflower rice.)

2. Heat the olive oil in a large wok or skillet over medium-high heat, for 1 to 2 minutes.

3. Add the cauliflower rice. Season with sea salt and black pepper.

4. Stir-fry for 3 to 5 minutes, uncovered, until cauliflower rice is soft but not mushy. (Think al dente.) Do not cover. (Frozen riced cauliflower may take a few minutes longer to cook.)

5. Adjust salt and pepper to taste if, desired.

NUTRITION INFO: 98 Calories | 7g Fat | 7g Total Carbs | 3g Fiber | 4g Net Carbs | 2g Protein

ESTIMATING HOW MUCH TO MAKE

A serving of white rice is ½ cup, but for cauliflower rice, 1 cup is more typical. Use this chart to find out how much cauliflower rice you'll get based on the size of your cauliflower head.

Cauliflower Head Size	Total Weight (with Leaves & Stems)	Volume of Cauliflower Rice	Weight of Cauliflower Rice
Medium	1½ pounds	4 cups	1 pound
Large	2 pounds	6 cups	1½ pounds
Extra Large	3 pounds	8 cups	2 pounds

MOST IMPORTANT TIPS

- **Use more florets and fewer stems.** You can still use the stems if you like, but the flavor and texture is better if you use mostly florets.
- **Avoid overcooking.** Make sure to watch your riced cauliflower during cooking, as it cooks fast and can get mushy quickly.
- **Don't cover it.** Leave the cover off so that the water can evaporate. When the pan is covered, you're essentially steaming the cauliflower, which increases its odor and makes it mushier, sometimes even watery. Stir-frying over higher heat is best.
- **Don't use water.** Do not cook riced cauliflower in water like you would normal rice. It will just get soggy.
- **Add to soups at the end.** If you are adding riced cauliflower to soup, add it at the end, so that it cooks for only a few minutes.
- **Precook for casseroles.** If you are using cauliflower in a casserole, it's best to cook it first to avoid a watery result.
- **Adjust sauce amounts.** Cauliflower rice does not soak up as much extra moisture as regular rice does, so you may need less sauce if you use it as a replacement in a recipe.

OTHER RICE ALTERNATIVES

While cauliflower rice is the most common and popular low carb rice substitute, there are a few others that sometimes work:

- **Shirataki rice:** Also called konjac rice, this is a natural, rice-shaped, plant-based low carb rice replacement, made from the fiber of the Japanese konjac plant. It's 97% water, 3% fiber, very low in carbs and calories, and naturally gluten-free. Some people find that it has an off-putting texture and/or flavor, but it can help to follow a process of rinsing well, boiling for a few minutes, and then frying in a dry pan for about 10 minutes. After that, you can use this rice the same way that you would use cooked white rice.
- **Cabbage rice:** Although cabbage is not really similar to rice, you can use finely chopped cooked cabbage (like a cooked slaw) in recipes to add bulk.
- **Hemp hearts:** If you're looking for a firmer texture than cauliflower rice, try cooking hemp hearts with water or broth, along with other vegetables that you like with rice. The hemp hearts will absorb liquid similarly to how rice would, though the texture is much finer.

POTATO SUBSTITUTES

Potatoes are pretty firmly off limits for keto lifestyle followers, but fortunately there are many vegetables that can be used to replace them. These range from very low carb varieties (like cauliflower) to those best enjoyed in moderation (like rutabagas), and higher carb options (like butternut squash) that really only work when combined with other, lower carb ingredients.

I'm all about variety, so this book has a little of almost everything, but many of these potato substitutes are actually interchangeable. For example, if a recipe calls for celery root, feel free to swap in radishes or turnips to fit your macro needs. Cook times vary a bit depending on the veggie, but the cooking methods are generally the same for most of them.

POTATO SUBSTITUTE	FLAVOR & BEST USES	TRY IT IN...
Radish 2g net carbs per cup	Spicy and zesty when raw, but mellow and nutty when cooked, with the appearance of red potatoes. Use anywhere you'd use cooked baby potatoes.	**Scalloped Radishes** (p. 81). Sub in **Rutabaga Chips** (p. 180), **Loaded Just-Like-Potato Salad** (p. 82), **Breakfast Sausage Hash** (p. 201)
Cauliflower 3.2g net carbs per cup	Neutral flavor and very versatile, but most similar to potatoes when mashed or pureed (especially in soups).	**Simple Mashed Cauliflower** (p. 77), **Faux Mashed Sweet Potatoes** (p. 70), **Crispy Baked Cauliflower Tots** (p. 86). Sub in **Breakfast Sausage Hash** (p. 201), **Scalloped Radishes** (p. 81), **Loaded Just-Like-Potato Salad** (p. 82).
Jicama 5.1g net carbs per cup	Root vegetable that tastes like a cross between a potato and an apple. The sweetness is subtle and easily masked with salt. Great for fries, potato salads, etc.	Sub in **Breakfast Sausage Hash** (p. 201), **Scalloped Radishes** (p. 81), **Loaded Just-Like-Potato Salad** (p. 82)
Turnip 6.1g net carbs per cup	Sweet, nutty, and earthy taste, with some flavor undertones similar to radishes and cabbage. Like rutabagas, you can use them for fries, mash, chips, or anywhere else you'd normally use potatoes.	Sub in **Breakfast Sausage Hash** (p. 201), **Loaded Just-Like-Potato Salad** (p. 82), **Scalloped Radishes** (p. 81)
Rutabaga 8.9g net carbs per cup	Tastes like a cross between potatoes and cabbage. Though carb count is moderate, rutabaga is my favorite potato replacement for taste and texture. Use for fries, mash, chips, and everything in between.	**Rutabaga Chips** (p. 180), **Rutabaga Fries** (p. 66), Sub in **Breakfast Sausage Hash** (p. 201), **Scalloped Radishe**s (p. 81), **Loaded Just-Like-Potato Salad** (p. 82)
Pumpkin 6.9g net carbs per cup	Sweet winter squash, commonly used as a puree. Most people think of pumpkin for baking, but it's a great addition to a mock sweet potato mash, too.	**Faux Mashed Sweet Potatoes** (p. 70)
Celery Root (Celeriac) 11.6g net carbs per cup	Bumpy, beige root vegetable that tastes similar to a white potato when cooked. Carb count is on the higher side, but it's great for mixing with other ingredients.	**Loaded Just-Like-Potato Salad** (p. 82), **Breakfast Sausage Hash,** (p. 201)
Butternut Squash 15g net carbs per cup	Sweet and nutty flavor. Too high in carbs on its own, but it can fit keto stovetop when blended with lower carb ingredients, such as cauliflower.	**Faux Mashed Sweet Potatoes** (p. 70)

PASTA SUBSTITUTES

Of all the carbs I miss on a low carb lifestyle, pasta is my greatest weakness — it was practically its own food group for me growing up. The good news is there are lots of ways we can make keto friendly noodles, minus the carb overload.

The simplest forms of low carb noodles are actually vegetables: zucchini noodles and spaghetti squash. Anyone who tells you that these taste exactly like pasta is either lying or might have forgotten what real pasta tastes like; however, they are absolutely delicious in their own right, and for me they do satisfy that craving for a noodle dish.

In this section, we'll cover the basics of cooking zoodles and spaghetti squash, as well as several less common pasta substitutes.

All that being said, this book has a recipe for 3-Ingredient Egg Noodles (page 114) for when you want a noodle that is actually pasta, even if it means a little more effort.

ZUCCHINI NOODLES

Zucchini noodles, sometimes called zoodles, are simply zucchini that has been spiralized (cut into thin strips, forming long spiral strands). They cook quickly, have a mild flavor, and are very low in carbs and calories. However, they release a lot of moisture, which can make dishes watery. (See the basic recipe on the next page for ways to mitigate this.)

WAYS TO MAKE ZOODLES

There are five different ways to make zoodles. I'll describe each for you, in order of my preference from the best to the worst:

1. **Countertop spiralizer:** By far my favorite! This method is super fast and makes zoodles that have uniform thickness. For best results, get a spiralizer that has a suction cup at the bottom to prevent it from sliding around on the counter. Once you secure it, cut off the ends of the zucchini, insert it horizontally into the spiralizer, and simply turn the crank, pushing the zucchini along toward the blade as you go, until the entire zucchini is spiralized.

2. **Handheld spiralizer:** This is a good option to save space in the kitchen, but requires more effort and tends to result in thinner zucchini noodles. To use, cut off the ends of the zucchini, insert one end into the spiralizer, and twist repeatedly with one hand while holding the spiralizer steady with the other.

3. **Julienne peeler:** A julienne peeler is one solution to avoid buying a separate tool, but it can be tedious and time-consuming. To use the julienne peeler, simply run it across the zucchini lengthwise, creating strands. Though it works, the zoodles sometimes come out uneven and it can be harder to make long strands.

4. **Buy:** Some grocery stores sell spiralized zucchini, ready to go. However, the fresh kind spoils very quickly and the frozen ones tend to come out very mushy.

5. **Knife:** This basically entails just cutting the zucchini into thin strips. It's definitely the most basic way to make zoodles, but it's also time-consuming and difficult to get thin enough noodles. Therefore, it is generally not recommended.

COUNTERTOP SPIRALIZER TIPS

- **Get a spiralizer that has a strong suction cup on the bottom.** It will save your sanity. I've tried several with the small suction cups, and they slide around.

- **Make sure the zucchini is centered on the spiralizer.** That way, you'll end up with more of the best zucchini noodles, which are the ones that include the edges and skin. The middle ones tend to be mushier. Also, this will help you avoid the super-short pieces that sometimes result when the zucchini isn't centered. You can always reposition it as you go along.
- **Choose zucchini with a smaller diameter when possible.** I prefer smaller zucchini for two reasons. First, you'll get more zoodles that include the skin, which are sturdier and release less water than the center ones. Second, small zucchini are less seedy.
- **Spiralize the zucchini raw and unpeeled, before cooking.** Peeled or cooked zucchini will not make it through the spiralizer.
- **Trim the spiralized zucchini length before cooking.** The strands can get very long, so snip them with kitchen shears if needed.

COOKING METHODS

No matter which recipe you want to make, in my testing, the best way to cook zucchini noodles was in the oven, and the next best was panfried. But to be thorough, I'll tell you about all the different ways to make them:

- **Stovetop:** Fry the zucchini noodles in a skillet. This is the most common method, but it's very easy for this method to come out watery (the recipe to the right avoids this).
- **Oven:** Bake zoodles on a sheet pan to draw out excess moisture. Surprisingly, this is the best method I've found. It requires no draining and no squeezing, yet the zoodles still turn out dry.
- **Raw:** Skip cooking altogether and swap in zucchini noodles for pasta in a cold salad.

BASIC ZUCCHINI NOODLES

SERVING SIZE 1 cup | SERVES 4

INGREDIENTS

20 ounces (about 4 medium) zucchini, spiralized
sea salt, for sprinkling, plus more to taste
2 tablespoons olive oil
black pepper, to taste

STOVETOP METHOD

1. Place zucchini noodles into a colander over the sink. Sprinkle with sea salt and toss. Let sit for 30 minutes to drain.

2. Squeeze the zoodles gently over the sink to release more water. No need to get out every last drop, just the majority.

3. Heat oil in a large sauté pan over medium-high heat. Add zucchini and stir-fry for 3 to 4 minutes, until al dente. (Cooking time may vary depending on how much zucchini you have and the size of your pan.) Season with black pepper and more sea salt to taste.

OVEN METHOD

1. Preheat the oven to 350 degrees F. Grease an extra large baking sheet. (Use parchment paper if it's not excellent non-stick.)

2. Arrange the zucchini on the baking sheet in a thin layer, making sure not to crowd the pan. Sprinkle lightly with sea salt, and toss.

3. Bake for about 15 minutes, until al dente. (You can cook longer if you want them softer.)

4. Pat the zoodles dry with a double layer of paper towels.

5. Toss with oil, black pepper, and more sea salt to taste, if needed.

NUTRITION INFO: 75 Calories | 6g Fat | 4g Total Carbs | 1g Fiber | 3g Net Carbs | 1g Protein

- **Boil or blanch:** Boil zoodles quickly. The end result is usually watery. Not necessarily right away, the zucchini will ooze water easily and quickly become too wet on your plate. Only use this method if you are making soup.
- **Microwave:** Heat zucchini noodles in the microwave. This can work in a pinch, but it's a lot harder to avoid making them watery. If you want to do it anyway, the best way is to follow the draining and squeezing method just like you would when panfrying (see recipe below), then microwave. You may still need to drain or pat away additional moisture afterward. Once the zucchini is hot, drain it and then add sauce.

SPAGHETTI SQUASH

Spaghetti squash is a unique type of winter squash that, when cooked, can be shredded into long strands that resemble spaghetti. These noodles have a neutral flavor, with subtle sweetness that is easily balanced by adding salt. Spaghetti squash can take longer to cook, but requires minimal effort.

COOKING METHODS

- **Halved in the oven:** Cut squash in half, then roast in the oven. This is the quickest oven method, but it can take some effort to cut the squash open—see the best way to do it below.
- **Whole in the oven:** Poke squash with a knife for venting and simply roast it whole. This takes longer, but is also less effort. It also has a more mild, neutral flavor than squash cut in half prior to roasting.
- **Microwave:** This is the fastest method, but also requires cutting the squash in half first. Also, some people may prefer not to cook with the microwave, and others may not like that

this method cooks the squash with moist heat.
- **Pressure cooker:** Cook whole on a trivet inside the pressure cooker along with water to essentially steam the squash. The cook time is usually very fast, but it takes a while to come up to pressure. This method is also not my favorite because it uses moist heat.
- **Slow cooker:** This method is easy because you simply poke holes in the squash, place it in the slow cooker, and wait for it to be done. Patience is not my strong suit, and unlike with other slow cooker recipes, there is no flavor benefit from slow cooking spaghetti squash, so it's not my top recommendation.

CUTTING TIPS

When your cooking method requires you to cut the spaghetti squash in half, it can be a little daunting. Here are some tricks to make it easier:
- **Score it first.** Cutting straight through the hard skin of an uncooked spaghetti squash can be very difficult, but if you make a dashed score line with your knife around the perimeter first, it's much easier.
- **Cut crosswise instead of lengthwise** if you want long strands. The strands run in circles perpendicular to the length of the squash, so you'll get longer strands if you cut it crosswise.
- **Precook whole for even less effort.** If you really want the benefits of cooking squash halved but don't want to fuss with cutting it, there's an easier way. Simply poke holes all over the whole squash, then place in the oven or microwave to cook (5 minutes in the microwave or 10 minutes in the oven at 350 degrees F). Take out the squash, cut in half (it should be much easier now), and then proceed with the halved methods on the next page.

BASIC SPAGHETTI SQUASH NOODLES

SERVING SIZE 1 cup | SERVES 4

INGREDIENTS

1 medium spaghetti squash

4 teaspoons olive oil

sea salt, to taste

HALVED OVEN METHOD

1. Preheat the oven to 425 degrees F. Line a baking sheet with foil.

2. Use a sharp chef's knife to slice the spaghetti squash in half. To make it easier, use the knife to score where you'll be cutting first, then slice. Cut crosswise for longer noodles, or lengthwise for shorter ones. Discard the seeds.

3. Drizzle the inside of the halves with olive oil. Season with sea salt.

4. Place the spaghetti squash halves onto the lined baking sheet, cut side down. Roast in the oven for 25 to 35 minutes, until a knife inserted into the squash goes in with just a little resistance.

5. Remove from the oven, flip the halves over, and rest for 10 minutes.

6. Use a fork to scrape the inside of the squash, perpendicular to its length, to release the strands.

WHOLE OVEN METHOD

1. Preheat the oven to 425 degrees F. Line a baking sheet with foil.

2. Use a sharp knife to poke holes in the spaghetti squash skin for venting steam.

3. Place the spaghetti squash onto the lined baking sheet. Roast in the oven for about 35 to 45 minutes, flipping over halfway through, until a knife inserted into the squash goes in with just a little resistance.

4. Remove from the oven, then rest 10 minutes before slicing. Cut the spaghetti squash in half crosswise for longer noodles, or lengthwise for shorter ones.

5. Scoop out the seeds, then use a fork to scrape the inside of the squash, perpendicular to its length, to release the strands. Toss with olive oil and sea salt

MICROWAVE METHOD

1. Use a sharp chef's knife to slice the spaghetti squash in half. To make it easier, use the knife to score where you'll be cutting first, then slice. Cut crosswise for longer noodles, or lengthwise for shorter ones. Discard the seeds.

2. Place the squash into a glass baking dish, cut side down, and add half an inch of water.

3. Microwave for 10 to 20 minutes, until a knife inserted into the squash goes in with just a little resistance.

4. Use a fork to scrape the inside of the squash, perpendicular to its length, to release the strands.

NUTRITION INFO: 75 Calories | 4g Fat | 10g Total Carbs | 2g Fiber | 8g Net Carbs | 1g Protein

OTHER PASTA SUBSTITUTES

If you get bored with squash, or simply want to try something different, you may want to experiment with other pasta alternatives. In fact, you can make almost any noodle recipe in this book using different types of noodles if you like.

- **Keto pasta noodles:** If you want to make an actual pasta instead of simply veggies in a noodle shape, I've found that lupin flour made into a mozzarella dough works best. Try it with 3-Ingredient Egg Noodles (page 114) or Classic Beef Lasagna (page 222).
- **Cabbage noodles:** Cabbage doesn't have the same flavor or texture that traditional noodles would, but if you slice it into long strands and sauté it, the flavor is delicious with many pasta sauces.
- **Shirataki noodles:** Sometimes called konjac noodles, these are made from the fiber of the Japanese konjac plant. Like shirataki rice, they are 97% water, 3% fiber, very low in carbs and calories, and naturally gluten-free. To avoid an undesirable texture or flavor, the best cooking process involves rinsing, boiling, and then frying in a dry pan. Try them in Vegetable Lo Mein (page 113).
- **Kelp noodles:** These clear, thin noodles are made from kelp, a brown seaweed. Their texture can be a little crunchy, but they soften when cooked.
- **Spiralized vegetables:** Don't limit yourself to zucchini noodles! Cucumbers, eggplant, and even kohlrabi can all be spiralized in the same way. Cucumber noodles are best enjoyed raw, eggplant is better cooked, and kohlrabi can go either way. **Get a full list of keto friendly veggies at www.wholesomeyum.com/ keto-vegetables.**

- **Cauliflower:** Although it's not even remotely reminiscent of a noodle, cauliflower often makes a good substitute for pasta in casseroles, as well as other dishes in which the sauce is the star or you need a neutral ingredient to add bulk. See for yourself with Cauliflower Carbonara (page 122), Cauliflower Baked "Ziti" (page 218), or Cauliflower Mac & Cheese (page 106).

FRIED FOOD SUBSTITUTES

Fried foods are deemed unhealthy by most diets, keto or not. The combination of high fat and high carbs together is simply not good for us, not to mention that deep frying is often done in industrial seed oils, which are highly processed, unstable, usually GMO, and too high in omega-6 fatty acids.

With a keto friendly breading and a healthy oil, though, it's possible to enjoy fried foods as part of a keto lifestyle. Remember, that doesn't mean that they should make up the bulk of what you eat, but you can enjoy them as a treat without derailing your efforts.

BREADING

Ingredients used for regular breading, such as breadcrumbs, crackers, or cornmeal, are not keto friendly at all, so we have to use alternatives. Just as combining flours is beneficial for low carb baking, using multiple ingredients is helpful for breading as well.

- **Crushed pork rinds:** Pork rinds are best known as a crunchy, salty, zero carb snack made from fried pigskins, but when you crush them, they are a perfect candidate for keto friendly breading. They are naturally crispy, which can be hard to come by with low carb breading options. Pork rinds can be used as breading on their own, but I prefer them mixed with almond flour so that their flavor is not overpowering. Also, although you can crush pork rinds using a zip-lock bag and a mallet, I always recommend doing so in a blender, because it's very fast and makes consistent, uniform pieces that are not too big or too small.
- **Almond flour:** Almond flour works fine as a lighter, thinner breading and works best when

THE BEST TECHNIQUE FOR BREADING

- **Prep dredging ingredient(s):** Place coconut flour or protein powder into a shallow bowl for dredging; you can usually start with ¼ or ½ cup for most recipes, as only a small amount will stick. If the food will need salt and pepper, I recommend adding them to the same bowl, so that they will be directly touching the food. Finely ground spices are also fine to add to the dredging bowl, or they can be added to the breading bowl instead.

- **Whisk eggs:** The number of eggs you need will depend on the size and quantity of the items you'll be breading. I usually start with one or two eggs and whisk more as needed.

- **Mix breading ingredient(s):** Choose pork rinds, almond flour, crushed nuts, or a combination of these and add any dried herbs and/or spices you like. A total volume of 1 to 2 cups is a good starting point for an average recipe.

- **Apply the breading:** Dredge the food pieces (chicken, fish, etc.) in the dredging mixture, dip in the eggs, gently shake off the excess, then press into the breading mixture. To prevent clumping, keep most of the breading mixture in a separate bowl and add a little at a time to the bowl where you'll be dipping.

For battered foods instead of breaded, use the technique described in the Deep-Fried Onion Rings recipe (page 149) instead.

frying. Baking items that have been breaded with almond flour tends to leave the breading fairly soft, though nonetheless delicious. However, almond flour combined with pork rinds makes an excellent crispy fried breading, and almond flour combined with whey protein powder makes an exceptional keto batter. For those who cannot have nuts, sunflower seed meal can be used in place of almond flour to make any breading or batter.

- **Whey protein powder:** This is one of my favorite keto friendly breading options, though it works best for battered foods (that is, foods coated in a wet batter and then deep-fried) rather than simply breaded. The result is very crispy and a bit airy, and the texture is best when combined with almond flour. Try it in Deep-Fried Onion Rings (page 149) and Fish & Chips (page 158). Unlike baking recipes where other protein powders can sometimes be substituted for whey protein powder, I don't recommend substitutions for battering, where most other varieties come out chewy instead of crispy. However, protein powder can also be used for dredging, and for that you can use any kind of unflavored protein powder.
- **Coconut flour:** Avoid using coconut flour alone to bread foods—the texture is too fine for a breading, and it's too absorbent for a batter. However, where coconut flour really shines is for dredging. It has a fine texture that adheres easily and helps to dry the surface of foods so that an egg wash can stick well.
- **Crushed nuts:** If you're looking for crunch but are not a fan of pork rinds, finely chopped or crushed nuts can be a good alternative for a very crispy exterior.

OILS

If your goal is clean keto, choosing a healthy oil to fry with is just as important as choosing a breading. First, make sure your oil has a high smoke point, which is the temperature at which a fat starts to burn and smoke. You don't want to exceed the smoke point while frying, because this causes the oil to become unstable, releases free radicals, and makes food taste burnt. Second, avoid industrial seed oils extracted from soybeans, corn, cottonseeds, safflower seeds, and rapeseeds. Even though these have a high smoke point, they are heated to extreme temperatures (causing oxidation), processed with solvent, bleached, and deodorized before they are bottled.

Below are the oils I recommend, and you can use any of them for any fried recipe in this book.

- **Avocado oil:** Refined avocado oil is one of the best oils for frying because it has the highest smoke point, between 510 and 520 degrees F. Unrefined, extra-virgin avocado oil has a smoke point of 480 degrees F and is fine to use as well, but you'll definitely notice an avocado flavor to it. All avocado oil is rich in vitamin E, antioxidants, and oleic acid, a monounsaturated omega-9 fatty acid.
- **Olive oil:** Olive oil is always a solid choice, though I prefer to stick to a refined, light, or virgin olive oil for frying, as this will have a higher smoke point than extra-virgin and is more neutral in flavor. The smoke point of olive oil ranges between 350 and 410 degrees F, depending on the type. Like avocado oil, olive oil is rich in vitamin E, antioxidants, and oleic acid.
- **Coconut oil:** Refined coconut oil has a smoke point of 400 degrees F and a neutral flavor, which means you can safely fry with it

without making your food taste like coconut. Unrefined virgin coconut oil has a lower smoke point (350 degrees F) and lots of coconut flavor, so it's best for lighter frying and only when coconut flavor is desirable. All coconut oil contains medium-chain triglycerides (MCTs), which are fatty acid chains that go straight to the liver for quick fat burning and ketone production—a great thing for a ketogenic lifestyle.

- **Lard or tallow:** Lard, tallow, and other animal fats have a smoke point of 374 degrees F and impart tons of flavor. This makes them great choices for deep-frying, where the typical intended temperature is around 350 degrees F. Avoid animal fats for high-temp cooking, such as searing a steak. Lard and tallow are good sources of vitamin D, choline, and oleic acid.

- **Ghee:** Although butter is not ideal for frying because it burns so easily, clarified butter (another name for ghee) has a very high smoke point at 482 degrees F. This makes it great for all kinds of high-heat cooking, from deep frying to searing. Ghee is rich in vitamins A, C, D, and K; omega-3 fatty acids; and beneficial conjugated linoleic acid.

BREAD

FLUFFY SOFT WHITE BREAD

SERVING SIZE 1 slice (½-inch thick) | **SERVES 18**

A common issue with keto breads is that they are dense and crumbly. Not this one! The whipped egg white technique here is similar to the technique used when making angel food cake and leaves us with a soft, airy, fluffy yet chewy white bread. At just 1.3g net carbs per slice, it's an ideal choice for sandwiches.

1 cup super fine blanched almond flour

¼ cup coconut flour

1 tablespoon Besti Monk Fruit Allulose Blend

2 teaspoons baking powder

¼ teaspoon xanthan gum

¼ teaspoon sea salt

5 tablespoons plus 1 teaspoon butter, melted

12 large egg whites, at room temperature (about 1½ cups)

¼ teaspoon cream of tartar, optional

STORAGE

Refrigerate for up to 5 days, wrapped in parchment paper. (Avoid plastic.)

Freeze for up to 4 months.

1. Preheat the oven to 325 degrees F. Line an 8½ x 4½-inch loaf pan with parchment paper, with extra hanging over the sides for easy removal later.

2. Combine the almond flour, coconut flour, Besti, baking powder, xanthan gum, and salt in a large food processor. Pulse until combined.

3. Add the melted butter. Pulse, scraping down the sides as needed, until crumbly.

4. In a very large bowl, use a hand mixer to beat the egg whites and cream of tartar, if using, until stiff peaks form. Make sure the bowl is large enough because the whites will expand a lot.

5. Add half of the stiff egg whites to the food processor. Pulse a few times, until just combined. Do not overmix!

6. Carefully transfer the mixture from the food processor into the bowl with the egg whites and gently fold, until no streaks remain. Do not stir. Fold gently to keep the mixture as fluffy as possible.

7. Transfer the batter to the lined loaf pan and smooth the top. Gently push the batter toward the center a bit to round the top.

8. Bake for about 40 minutes, until the top is golden brown. Tent with aluminum foil and bake for another 30 to 45 minutes, until the top is firm and does not make a squishy sound when pressed. Cool completely before removing from the pan and slicing.

Unlock this recipe in the Easy Keto App

NUTRITION INFO: 83 Calories | 6.8g Fat | 2.6g Total Carbs | 1.3g Fiber | 1.3g Net Carbs | 3.8g Protein

TIPS & VARIATIONS

- For a dairy-free version, substitute unrefined coconut oil for the butter.

- If you don't think you'll have a use for the 12 yolks that will be left over, feel free to use carton egg whites. Note that they may take a bit longer to form stiff peaks.

- The key to making this bread fluffy is to whip the whites well and avoid breaking them down when folding with the other ingredients. (Cream of tartar helps with this, so use it if you have it.) The whites are what creates the lift and bulk of the bread.

- This bread may hold some extra moisture the day you make it, but will dry to optimal consistency by the next day. You can toast it to further improve texture.

GARLIC PARMESAN BISCUITS

SERVING SIZE 1 biscuit | **SERVES 16**

Garlic Parmesan biscuits are the perfect pairing for a soup, salad, or even keto friendly pasta (see Pasta substitutes, page 105). They are buttery, aromatic, and quick to throw together.

1. Preheat the oven to 350 degrees F. Line a baking sheet with parchment paper.

2. In a large bowl, stir together the almond flour, baking powder, garlic powder, and salt.

3. Stir in the egg, heavy cream, and melted butter until uniform. Fold in ¾ cup of the Parmesan.

4. Use a medium cookie scoop (1½ to 2 tablespoons in size) to scoop the dough onto the prepared baking sheet, at least 1½ inches apart, for a total of 16 biscuits. Form into rounded biscuit shapes, flattening slightly with your hands to about ½-inch thickness.

5. Sprinkle each biscuit with ½ teaspoon of Parmesan, using up the remaining ½ cup of the cheese.

6. Bake for about 15 minutes, until golden. Cool for 10 to 15 minutes without moving, to firm up.

7. Stir together all the topping ingredients. Brush the biscuits with the melted butter topping right before serving.

BISCUITS

2 cups super fine blanched almond flour

2 teaspoons baking powder

2 teaspoons garlic powder

⅛ teaspoon sea salt

1 large egg, whisked

⅓ cup heavy cream

⅓ cup butter, melted

1¼ cups shredded Parmesan cheese, divided (¾ cup and ½ cup)

TOPPING

3 tablespoons butter, melted

1 tablespoon fresh parsley, chopped

¼ teaspoon garlic powder

⅛ teaspoon sea salt, or to taste

STORAGE

Refrigerate for up to 5 days.

Freeze for up to 6 months.

VARIATIONS

- For a different flavor profile, feel free to swap the Parmesan with another hard cheese, such as Asiago, Pecorino Romano, Gruyere, or Cheddar.

- Parsley can be replaced with other fresh herbs, such as rosemary or thyme.

NUTRITION INFO: 190 Calories | 17.6g Fat | 3.7g Total Carbs | 1.6g Fiber | 2.1g Net Carbs | 6.5g Protein

Unlock this recipe in the Easy Keto App

NUT FREE OPTION

VEGETARIAN

SOFT PRETZELS

SERVING SIZE 1 pretzel | **SERVES 6**

These keto soft pretzels remind me of trips to the mall as a teenager, where I'd always get a soft pretzel with cheese dipping sauce from the soft pretzel shop. In this recipe, you'll find the same chewy texture, irresistible yeast flavor, and even the coarse salt topping of a classic mall pretzel.

1½ cups super fine blanched almond flour

½ tablespoon baking powder

1 packet (2¼ teaspoons) instant yeast

1 teaspoon inulin powder

¼ teaspoon xanthan gum

2 large eggs

3 cups shredded mozzarella cheese

1 ounce cream cheese, cubed

Avocado oil cooking spray

2 teaspoons coarse pretzel salt

STORAGE

Refrigerate for up to 5 days.

Freeze for up to 6 months.

1. Place the almond flour, baking powder, instant yeast, inulin powder, xanthan gum, and eggs into a food processor. Pulse until uniform.

2. In a medium bowl, combine the mozzarella and cream cheese. Heat in the microwave for about 90 seconds, or in a double boiler on the stove, until melted. Stir until smooth and uniform.

3. Add the cheese mixture to the food processor, positioning the cheese so that the blades are sticking into it. Process until a uniform dough forms, scraping the sides with a spatula, if necessary.

4. Form the dough into a ball, cover, and place in a warm place (like a turned off oven with the light on) for 1 hour. After that, if the dough is sticky, cover with plastic and refrigerate for 30 minutes.

5. Preheat the oven to 400 degrees F. Line a large baking sheet with parchment paper.

6. Cut the ball of dough into 6 sections, like a pie. Using oiled hands, roll each section into a long, skinny log, about 18 inches long. Twist into a pretzel shape by taking one end of the dough and looping it around and down across the bottom, then repeat with the other end, crossing over the first. Place onto the baking sheet. Repeat with the remaining dough sections.

7. Spray the pretzels lightly with avocado oil spray. Sprinkle coarse salt over them and press gently.

8. Bake for 10 to 12 minutes, until golden.

Unlock this recipe in the Easy Keto App
←

NUTRITION INFO: 350 Calories | 26.3g Fat | 9.3g Total Carbs | 3.9g Fiber | 5.4g Net Carbs | 22.9g Protein

TIPS & VARIATIONS

- For a nut-free version, replace the 1½ cups of almond flour with just 6 tablespoons of coconut flour. (You'll end up with fewer pretzels.)

- Inulin powder is a prebiotic that feeds the yeast. If you can't find it, you can also use regular white sugar or coconut sugar; the yeast will consume most of it, so the final nutrition info won't be significantly affected.

- Want an easy cheese dipping sauce to go with your soft pretzel? Find the recipe at: **www.wholesomeyum.com/ low-carb-keto-cheese- sauce-recipe**.

SKILLET CORNBREAD

SERVING SIZE 1 slice, or ¹⁄₁₆ entire recipe (it's very filling, so we cut it into 16 slices) | **SERVES 16**

Corn is too high in carbs to be used in keto recipes, but we can still get the same flavor, thanks to sweet corn extract. This skillet cornbread is soft, moist, and buttery, with a tender crumb. It's the perfect pairing for a warm bowl of soup.

1. Preheat the oven to 400 degrees F. Grease a 10-inch cast iron skillet with butter.

2. In a large bowl, stir together the almond flour, baking powder, Besti, and salt.

3. Stir in the melted butter, almond milk, and eggs until smooth. Stir in the sweet corn extract.

4. Transfer the batter into the skillet and smooth the top with a spatula. Bake for 35 to 40 minutes, until an inserted toothpick comes out clean and the top is golden brown.

5 cups super fine blanched almond flour

1 tablespoon baking powder

¹⁄₃ cup Besti Monk Fruit Allulose Blend

1 teaspoon sea salt

²⁄₃ cup butter, melted, plus more for greasing

²⁄₃ cup unsweetened almond milk

6 large eggs, whisked

1 tablespoon sweet corn extract

STORAGE

Store on the counter for 1 to 2 days.

Refrigerate for up to 5 days.

Freeze for up to 6 months.

TIPS & VARIATIONS

• This cornbread is lightly sweet. For sweeter cornbread, increase the amount of Besti to ½ cup, or ²⁄₃ cup for extra sweet.

• Sweet corn extract can be found in the baking aisle at the grocery store or online. You can omit it if you can't find it, but you'll lose the corn flavor in the final bread.

• For a dairy-free version, substitute coconut oil for the butter. Since a buttery flavor is a major component of cornbread, consider using butter-flavored coconut oil, but any unrefined variety will work.

NUTRITION INFO: 297 Calories | 27.1g Fat | 8g Total Carbs | 3.8g Fiber | 4.2g Net Carbs | 10g Protein

Unlock this recipe in the Easy Keto App

BREAD

SECRET INGREDIENT BANANA BREAD

SERVING SIZE 1 slice (about ¾ inch thick) | **SERVES 12**

When I first embarked on a low carb lifestyle, bananas were one of the fruits I missed the most. I quickly discovered that using its natural extract—the secret ingredient in this banana bread—in baking fulfills that craving beautifully. This bread is moist and sweet and brimming with banana flavor, so you'd never guess there are no bananas in it.

2 cups super fine blanched almond flour

¼ cup coconut flour

1 tablespoon baking powder

2 teaspoons cinnamon

½ teaspoon xanthan gum

¼ teaspoon sea salt

½ cup butter, softened

⅔ cup Besti Monk Fruit Allulose Blend

4 large eggs, at room temperature

½ cup unsweetened almond milk, at room temperature

2 teaspoons banana extract

1 cup chopped walnuts, divided (¾ cup and ¼ cup), optional

STORAGE

Store on the counter for 1 to 2 days.

Refrigerate for up to 5 days.

Freeze for up to 6 months.

1. Preheat the oven to 350 degrees F. Line an 8½ x 4½-inch loaf pan with parchment paper, with extra hanging over the sides for easy removal later.

2. In a large bowl, mix together the almond flour, coconut flour, baking powder, cinnamon, xanthan gum, and salt.

3. In another large bowl, use a hand mixer to beat butter and Besti, until fluffy.

4. In the same bowl with the butter, beat in the eggs, one at a time, followed by the almond milk and banana extract.

5. With the mixer running at medium speed, gradually add the dry ingredients into the wet and mix, until thick and uniform.

6. Stir in ¾ cup of the chopped walnuts, if using.

7. Transfer the batter into the lined loaf pan and press evenly to make a smooth top. Sprinkle the top with the remaining ¼ cup of the chopped walnuts, if using, and press them lightly into the surface.

8. Bake for 30 to 40 minutes, until the top is golden. Tent the top with foil and then bake for 20 to 25 more minutes, until an inserted toothpick comes out clean.

9. Cool completely before removing from the pan and slicing.

Unlock this recipe in the Easy Keto App

NUTRITION INFO: 212 Calories | 19.1g Fat | 6.4g Total Carbs | 3.2g Fiber | 3.2g Net Carbs | 6.6g Protein

Nutrition info does not include the optional walnuts.

TIPS & VARIATIONS

- For a dairy-free version, use unrefined coconut oil instead of butter.

- The longer you let the bread sit before slicing, the better it will hold together; the next day is ideal, if possible.

- Try swapping the walnuts with other chopped nuts (pecans, almonds, etc.), sugar-free chocolate chips, or small amounts of dried berries (be sure there is no sugar added).

- You can make a glaze topping by whisking together ¼ cup Besti Powdered Monk Fruit Allulose Blend, 1 to 2 tablespoons heavy cream, and vanilla extract to taste.

TIPS & VARIATIONS

- If you are not dairy-free, replace the coconut cream and mayonnaise with cream cheese, which produces a slightly better texture.

- The most important aspect of this recipe is to keep the egg whites airy and not break them down during folding. When you make the discs on the parchment paper, the batter should be fluffy, not runny.

- Humidity can affect whipped egg whites. Your cloud bread always will be delicious, but may be less fluffy if your environment is humid.

DAIRY-FREE CLOUD BREAD

SERVING SIZE 1 cloud bread | **SERVES 6**

Cloud bread, traditionally made with separated eggs and cream cheese, is one of the few keto breads that doesn't require any kind of flour. It's very light and airy, and much lower in calories and carbs than most low carb bread options. The only problem is it has been inaccessible to my dairy-free readers, so I created this recipe for them to enjoy as well. (If you do eat dairy, see the tips for how to make the original.)

1. The night before making cloud bread, place an unopened can of coconut cream to the refrigerator. This will separate the cream from the water in the can, which is very important. The day of, skim ¼ cup of the thick cream on top to use in the recipe.

2. Preheat the oven to 300 degrees F. Line a baking sheet with parchment paper.

3. In a large bowl, use an electric mixer with a whisk attachment to beat the egg whites and cream of tartar, until stiff peaks form.

4. Change the mixer attachment to beaters. In a second large bowl, use the mixer to beat the yolks, mayonnaise, coconut cream, flaxseed meal, and salt, until smooth.

5. Gently and gradually fold the egg whites into the yolk mixture with a large spatula, until just combined. Be careful to avoid breaking down the whites. Do not stir.

6. Scoop the mixture into six circular discs onto the parchment paper, at least 1½ inches apart. Bake for 25 to 30 minutes, until golden.

¼ cup coconut cream

3 large eggs, yolks and whites separated

⅛ teaspoon cream of tartar

2 tablespoons avocado oil mayonnaise

1 tablespoon golden flaxseed meal

⅛ teaspoon sea salt

STORAGE

Refrigerate for up to 5 days.

Freeze for up to 6 months.

Unlock this recipe in the Easy Keto App

NUTRITION INFO: 111 Calories | 10.2g Fat | 1.4g Total Carbs | 0.7g Fiber | 0.7g Net Carbs | 3.8g Protein

BREAD

SOFT SANDWICH BUNS & ROLLS

SERVING SIZE 1 roll or bun | **SERVES 6**

These soft rolls are the ideal accompaniment to pretty much anything that goes on a bun: burgers, brats, hot dogs, subs, you name it. Thanks to the whey protein powder that creates structure and psyllium husk powder for the perfect chew, this dough is pleasant to work with, rises beautifully, and creates an unmatched soft, airy result.

1 cup super fine blanched almond flour

¼ cup whey protein powder

3 tablespoons psyllium husk powder

1 tablespoon baking powder

½ teaspoon sea salt

2 tablespoons avocado oil

1 tablespoon apple cider vinegar

3 large egg whites

1 cup boiling water

STORAGE

Refrigerate for up to 5 days.

Freeze for up to 6 months.

1. Preheat the oven to 350 degrees F. Line a baking sheet with parchment paper.

2. In a large bowl, stir together the almond flour, whey protein powder, psyllium husk powder, baking powder, and salt.

3. Add the avocado oil, apple cider vinegar, and egg whites. Stir until uniform.

4. Pour in the boiling water slowly while beating with a hand mixer at low speed for about 1 minute. The dough will absorb the water. Do not overmix. At this point, the dough will be a little wet, so let it sit for 5 minutes to thicken. (You can also refrigerate for 10 minutes to help it thicken.)

5. Cut the dough into 6 sections, like a pie. Use oiled hands to form a ball of dough from each section and place onto the baking sheet, 2 inches apart.

6. Bake for 25 to 30 minutes, until dark golden brown. Cool buns for at least 15 minutes before slicing.

Unlock this recipe in the Easy Keto App

NUTRITION INFO: 182 Calories | 14g Fat | 8.7g Total Carbs | 5.5g Fiber | **3.2g Net Carbs** | 8.1g Protein

TIPS & VARIATIONS

- If your kitchen is warm, the dough may be too sticky or too runny, so it can help to chill the dough for 20 minutes before forming it into balls.

- For a nut-free version, swap the almond flour with sunflower seed meal.

- For a dairy-free version, substitute egg white protein powder for the whey protein powder.

- Try topping the rolls with seasonings! Brush the rolls with egg wash and sprinkle on your toppings, such as sesame seeds or everything seasoning, before baking.

- To make oblong buns for subs, hot dogs, or brats, divide the dough into 4 sections instead of 6 and roll into a log shape before baking. Try it with Italian Meatball Subs (page 56).

TIPS & VARIATIONS

- For a dairy-free version, replace the whey protein powder with egg white protein powder.

- Inulin powder is a prebiotic that feeds the yeast. If you can't find it, you can also use regular white sugar or coconut sugar; the yeast will consume most of it, so the final nutrition info won't be significantly affected.

- The olive oil you choose will really shine here, so use the highest quality you can get. Be sure it's extra-virgin for maximum flavor.

- Feel free to add other herbs, such as parsley, thyme, oregano, basil, or marjoram, to your liking.

- Keto focaccia is very filling. The thickness as written is great for enjoying alongside a soup or salad, but if you want to make a sandwich, you may want to make it into a larger circle or rectangle, ¼ inch thick, for thinner slices.

ROSEMARY FOCACCIA

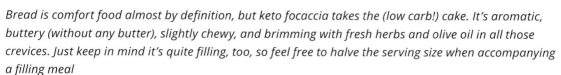

SERVING SIZE 1 slice, or ⅛ entire recipe | **SERVES 8**

Bread is comfort food almost by definition, but keto focaccia takes the (low carb!) cake. It's aromatic, buttery (without any butter), slightly chewy, and brimming with fresh herbs and olive oil in all those crevices. Just keep in mind it's quite filling, too, so feel free to halve the serving size when accompanying a filling meal

1. In a small bowl, stir together the warm water, inulin powder, and active dry yeast. Set aside for 10 to 15 minutes to bloom.

2. In a large bowl, stir together the almond flour, whey protein powder, psyllium husk powder, salt, and xanthan gum.

3. Add the yeast mixture and ½ cup olive oil to the flour bowl. Beat using a hand mixer on low speed, until a uniform, wet dough forms.

4. Form the dough into a ball in the bowl. Cover with plastic wrap and place the bowl in a warm place to let the dough rise until it doubles in size, at least 1 hour.

5. Meanwhile, preheat the oven to 400 degrees F. Line a baking sheet with parchment paper.

6. Once the dough is done rising, place it onto the lined pan and flatten into a circular disk, about ½ inch thick and 8 inches in diameter.

7. Use spread fingers to poke holes in the surface of the dough, ½ inch apart, reaching the bottom of the baking sheet. Drizzle with 2 tablespoons of olive oil, then sprinkle with garlic powder and rosemary.

8. Bake for 10 to 12 minutes, until the focaccia is golden brown on top. Cool for 5 to 10 minutes to firm up.

½ cup warm water

1 teaspoon inulin powder

1 packet (2¼ teaspoons) active dry yeast

2 cups super fine blanched almond flour

½ cup whey protein powder

3 tablespoons psyllium husk powder

½ teaspoon sea salt

¼ teaspoon xanthan gum

½ cup plus 2 tablespoons extra-virgin olive oil, divided

½ teaspoon garlic powder

1 tablespoon fresh rosemary

STORAGE

Refrigerate for up to 5 days.

Freeze for up to 6 months.

NUTRITION INFO: 346 Calories | 31.7g Fat | 10g Total Carbs | 6.3g Fiber | 3.7g Net Carbs | 9.9g Protein

Unlock this recipe in the Easy Keto App

BREAD

45

90-SECOND FLAX BREAD

SERVING SIZE 1 ramekin (2 slices) | **SERVES 2**

If you haven't heard of 90-second bread before, it's exactly what it sounds like: bread that takes just 90 seconds to bake in the microwave—or a bit longer if you prefer the oven. With just five basic keto pantry ingredients (plus salt), this one is easy to throw together quickly when a craving strikes, and the inclusion of flaxseed meal makes the end result both chewy and sturdy.

1 tablespoon butter

3 tablespoons super fine blanched almond flour

1 teaspoon golden flaxseed meal

½ teaspoon baking powder

1 pinch sea salt

1 large egg

STORAGE

Refrigerate for up to 5 days.
Freeze for up to 6 months.

1. Melt the butter in a small bowl in the microwave, or in a small saucepan on the stove.

2. Stir in almond flour, flaxseed meal, baking powder, salt, and egg. Mix well until smooth and uniform.

3. Divide the batter into two ramekins, 3½ to 4 inches in diameter. Level the tops with the back of a spoon.

4. **Microwave method:** Microwave for about 90 seconds, until firm. **Oven method:** Preheat the oven to 350 degrees F. Bake for 10 to 15 minutes, until firm.

5. Run a knife around the inside of the ramekins and then flip onto a plate or paper towel to release. Slice in half.

TIPS & VARIATIONS

• For even better texture, toast bread slices in the toaster.

• For a dairy-free version, use coconut oil instead of butter.

• For a nutty version, stir a teaspoon each of whole golden flaxseeds and chopped nuts of your choice into the batter.

Unlock this recipe in the Easy Keto App

NUTRITION INFO: 151 Calories | 13.8g Fat | 2.6g Total Carbs | 1.5g Fiber | 1.1g Net Carbs | 5.5g Protein

TIPS & VARIATIONS

- Inulin powder is a prebiotic that feeds the yeast. If you can't find it, you can use regular white sugar or coconut sugar; the yeast will consume most of it, so the final nutrition info won't be significantly affected.

- Be sure your whey protein powder has zero carbs and sugar, otherwise they can add up fast in this recipe.

- Be careful not to underbake the bread, or it will collapse. Open the oven very briefly (don't remove the loaf) to check for doneness with a toothpick, as the bread can fall quickly if exposed to a reduced temperature before it's done.

- For added shine, brush the loaf with an egg wash before baking. You can also sprinkle sesame seeds or other seasonings you like over the egg wash.

- This bread is even better toasted! Pop the slices in the toaster if you have time.

PERFECT YEAST BREAD

SERVING SIZE 1 slice, ½ inch thick | **SERVES 16**

This yeast bread recipe is based on my Soft Sandwich Buns & Rolls (page 42), with yeast added and adjusted to work for a big, tall loaf. It took me eleven rounds of testing to get this one just right, and it was so worth it!

1. In a large bowl, stir together the almond flour, whey protein powder, psyllium husk powder, Besti, baking powder, instant yeast, inulin powder, and salt.

2. Mix in the avocado oil, apple cider vinegar, and egg whites, until uniform.

3. Pour in the boiling water while beating with a hand mixer at low speed for about 1 minute. Do not overmix.

4. Cover the bowl with plastic and set in a warm place, such as inside a turned off oven or microwave, to rise for 1 hour.

5. Preheat the oven to 325 degrees F. (If you used the oven to let the dough rise, remove the bowl before preheating.) Line an 8 x 4-inch loaf pan with parchment paper, with extra hanging over the sides for easy removal later.

6. Gently transfer the dough to the pan, being careful not to break down the air bubbles. Gently smooth the top with a spatula.

7. Bake for 30 to 35 minutes, until the top is golden brown. Tent the top with foil and continue baking for 20 to 30 minutes, until the top forms a dark brown hard crust and an inserted toothpick comes out clean.

8. Let the bread cool for 20 minutes in the pan, then lift by the edges of the parchment paper and cool completely on a wire rack before slicing.

2 cups super fine blanched almond flour

1⅔ cups whey protein powder

¼ cup plus 2 tablespoons psyllium husk powder

1½ tablespoons Besti Monk Fruit Allulose Blend

1½ tablespoons baking powder

2 teaspoons instant yeast

1½ teaspoons inulin powder

¼ teaspoon sea salt

3½ tablespoons avocado oil

2 tablespoons apple cider vinegar

6 large egg whites

1½ cups boiling water

STORAGE

Refrigerate for up to 5 days, wrapped in parchment paper. (Avoid plastic.)

Freeze for up to 6 months.

NUTRITION INFO: 156 Calories | 10.2g Fat | 7.5g Total Carbs | 4.8g Fiber | 2.7g Net Carbs | 10.8g Protein

Unlock this recipe in the Easy Keto App

BREAD

SOUPS & SANDWICHES

CAPRESE AVOCADO GRILLED CHEESE

SERVING SIZE 1 grilled cheese sandwich | **SERVES 1**

With gooey cheese and a major dose of carbs, a grilled cheese sandwich is the epitome of childhood foods for many. But that doesn't mean it doesn't have its place in adulthood—or on a keto diet. This caprese version is grilled cheese all grown up, complete with buttery bread.

2 slices Perfect Yeast Bread (page 49)

2 teaspoons butter

2 ounces fresh mozzarella, sliced thinly

½ medium roma tomato, sliced thinly

¼ medium avocado, sliced thinly

2 tablespoons packed fresh basil leaves

1 teaspoon balsamic glaze, no sugar added

1 teaspoon olive oil

STORAGE

Refrigerate for up to 1 day.

Freeze for up to 3 months, if made without avocado and basil.

1. Lay out two slices of the bread and spread butter on one side of each.

2. Stack ingredients in this order to make a sandwich: 1 slice of bread (buttered side down), mozzarella slices, tomatoes, avocado, basil, balsamic glaze, and the remaining slice of bread (buttered side up).

3. Heat olive oil in a small skillet over medium-low heat. Place the sandwich onto the skillet and cover with a lid. Cook for 2 to 3 minutes, until browned on the bottom. Carefully flip and cook for 2 to 3 minutes, until browned on the other side.

TIPS & VARIATIONS

• This recipe makes a very filling sandwich using ½-inch-thick slices of Perfect Yeast Bread (page 49). If you want to lighten up the carbs and calories, simply slice the bread a bit thinner or cut the sandwich serving size in half.

• If you can't find balsamic glaze without sugar added, it's easy to make your own: Heat balsamic vinegar in a small saucepan for about 20 minutes, until volume is reduced by half and consistency is thickened.

• Want to change up your grilled cheese? Use the same bread and cheese amounts and replace the fillings:
  ▸ **Cheddar Bacon Tomato:** bacon, sliced tomatoes, Cheddar
  ▸ **Three Cheese:** Cheddar, American, and mozzarella cheeses
  ▸ **Pesto:** pesto sauce, provolone, and fresh basil
  ▸ **Mexican:** avocado, jalapeños, and Mexican cheese blend
  ▸ **French Onion:** caramelized onions and Gruyere
  ▸ **Pizza:** marinara sauce, mozzarella, and pepperoni

Unlock this recipe in the Easy Keto App

NUTRITION INFO: 642 Calories | 49.6g Fat | 23.4g Total Carbs | 13.5g Fiber | 9.9g Net Carbs | 32.6g Protein

TIPS & VARIATIONS

- If the soup is too thick for your liking, you can add more broth and/or cream at the end, then adjust salt and pepper again as needed.

- Carrots are not keto friendly on their own, but are typically fine in small amounts in recipes like this one. If you prefer to avoid them, you can omit or replace them with diced bell peppers instead.

- For a dairy-free version, use coconut oil instead of butter and full-fat coconut milk in place of heavy cream.

- For a vegetarian version, use vegetable broth instead of chicken broth.

CAULIFLOWER WILD RICE SOUP

SERVING SIZE 1 cup | **SERVES 4**

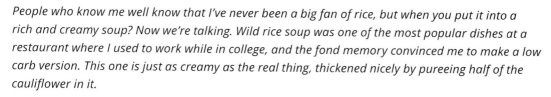

People who know me well know that I've never been a big fan of rice, but when you put it into a rich and creamy soup? Now we're talking. Wild rice soup was one of the most popular dishes at a restaurant where I used to work while in college, and the fond memory convinced me to make a low carb version. This one is just as creamy as the real thing, thickened nicely by pureeing half of the cauliflower in it.

1. In a large Dutch oven over high heat, combine the chicken broth and heavy cream. Bring to a boil, then reduce heat and simmer for 15 minutes.

2. Add half of the cauliflower rice. Simmer for 2 to 4 minutes, until cauliflower rice is soft.

3. Transfer the soup to a blender. Blend until smooth.

4. Wipe down the Dutch oven with a paper towel. Over medium heat, melt the butter. Add the onion, celery, carrots, garlic, and thyme. Cook for 7 to 10 minutes, until vegetables are soft.

5. Pour the pureed cauliflower and broth mixture back into the Dutch oven. Add the remaining cauliflower rice. Bring back to a boil and simmer for 2 to 4 minutes, until cauliflower rice is soft.

6. Season with salt and pepper to taste.

2 cups chicken broth

1 cup heavy cream

1 pound (4 cups) cauliflower rice, fresh or frozen, divided in half

1 tablespoon butter

½ large onion, diced

⅓ cup diced celery

⅓ cup diced carrots

3 cloves garlic, minced

1 tablespoon fresh thyme leaves

¾ teaspoon sea salt, or to taste

⅛ teaspoon black pepper, or to taste

STORAGE

Refrigerate for up to 5 days.

Freeze for up to 3 months.

Reheat very gently and stir to avoid separation.

NUTRITION INFO: 282 Calories | 25.1g Fat | 11.9g Total Carbs | 3.3g Fiber | 8.6g Net Carbs | 4.9g Protein

Unlock this recipe in the Easy Keto App

ITALIAN MEATBALL SUBS

SERVING SIZE 1 meatball sub | **SERVES 4**

What's more comforting than Italian meatballs with naturally sweet marinara sauce and gooey cheese? Stuffing them in a soft bun does the trick. These Italian meatball subs have all the saucy, beefy and cheesy filling you love, and most important, buns that taste just like wheat bread.

MEATBALLS

¼ cup super fine blanched almond flour

½ tablespoon Italian seasoning

½ teaspoon sea salt

¼ teaspoon black pepper

2 tablespoons heavy cream

2 tablespoons grated onion

1 large egg

2 cloves garlic, minced

½ pound ground beef

ASSEMBLY

4 Soft Sandwich Buns & Rolls (page 42), entire recipe made into 4 long sub shapes instead of 6 round buns

1 cup marinara sauce

1 cup shredded mozzarella cheese

STORAGE

Store meatballs and buns separately.

Refrigerate for up to 5 days.

Freeze for up to 6 months.

MEATBALLS

1. Preheat the oven to 400 degrees F. Line a baking sheet with foil or parchment paper.

2. In a large bowl, stir together the almond flour, Italian seasoning, salt, and pepper.

3. Whisk in the heavy cream, grated onion, egg, and garlic.

4. Mix in the ground beef using your hands, until just incorporated. Do not overmix, or else the meatballs may come out tough.

5. Form the mixture into 12 balls, about 1¼ to 1½ inches in diameter, and place on the prepared baking sheet.

6. Bake for 10 to 12 minutes, until the meatballs are cooked through. Leave the oven on at 400 degrees F.

ASSEMBLY

1. In a large sauté pan over medium-high heat, heat the marinara sauce, until simmering.

2. Add the meatballs and gently coat in sauce. Simmer for 3 to 4 minutes.

3. Slice the rolls in half and place onto a sheet pan. Fill each with 3 meatballs, then top each with marinara sauce from the pan and ¼ cup mozzarella.

4. Return to the oven for 3 to 5 minutes, until the cheese is melted.

Unlock this recipe in the Easy Keto App

NUTRITION INFO: 662 Calories | 47.8g Fat | 22.2g Total Carbs | 10.5g Fiber | 11.7g Net Carbs | 41.7g Protein

TIPS & VARIATIONS

• A medium cookie scoop (1½ to 2 tablespoons in size) works well for forming the meatballs. If using your hands, use a gentle touch and don't pack the meatballs too tightly.

• If you prefer your meatballs more golden, you can place them under the broiler for a couple of minutes after baking or panfry them for a few minutes over medium-high heat.

• These Italian meatballs with marinara sauce are also delicious served over noodles. Try Basic Zucchini Noodles (page 21), Basic Spaghetti Squash Noodles (page 23), or keto 3-Ingredient Egg Noodles (page 114).

TIPS & VARIATIONS

- If you prefer the feel of a true burger bun, use my Soft Sandwich Buns & Rolls recipe (page 42.

- Feel free to mix up the burger toppings with any of your favorites! Sugar-Free Ketchup (page 251) or mayonnaise can also be added instead of burger sauce.

- If you like, add a kick to your burger sauce with a pinch of cayenne pepper or sriracha.

- For a dairy-free version, omit the cheese.

BACON CHEESEBURGERS

SERVING SIZE 1 burger | SERVES 4

A lettuce-wrapped burger is a popular low carb option, but a common struggle is that they fall apart easily. Avoid this issue by using my technique with iceberg lettuce and skewers to hold your burgers together! These bacon cheeseburgers are piled high with toppings and dressed with a sweet burger sauce—you won't even miss the bread.

1. In a large skillet over medium heat, cook the bacon for about 10 minutes, turning halfway through, until crispy.

2. Meanwhile, in a large bowl, mix together the ground beef, salt, and pepper. Form into 4 patties, about ½ to ¾ inch thick. Make a thumbprint in each.

3. When the bacon is done, drain on paper towels, and wipe down the pan.

4. Heat the skillet over medium-high heat. Add the burger patties, cover, and cook for 4 to 5 minutes, until browned on the bottom and visible juices are no longer red. (Do not push down on the burgers or move them around.) Flip and cook 2 to 3 minutes for medium, or until done as desired. Add the cheese during the last minute and cover to melt. Remove from the pan, cover, and set aside to rest for 5 minutes.

5. Meanwhile, whisk together the mayonnaise, ketchup, garlic powder, and smoked paprika to make the burger sauce.

6. Cut off the hard end of the iceberg lettuce. Cut into 4 wedges (each wedge will be used to make a lettuce bun). Remove the small inner leaves, then divide the outer leaves evenly into 2 groups to use as top and bottom buns.

7. To assemble burgers, place a burger patty with cheese onto a lower lettuce bun, with the leaves curved upward. Top with bacon, avocado, tomato slices, avocado, a tablespoon of burger sauce, and finally the top lettuce bun, with the leaves curved downward. For easier handling, secure with a skewer.

NUTRITION INFO: 634 Calories | 49.7g Fat | 6.5g Total Carbs | 2.8g Fiber | 3.7g Net Carbs | 40.3g Protein

Nutrition info includes only about ⅔ small head iceberg lettuce, as the inner leaves are not used.

BURGERS

4 slices bacon

1 pound ground beef

1 teaspoon sea salt

¼ teaspoon black pepper

4 slices Cheddar cheese

½ medium avocado, sliced thinly

2 medium roma tomatoes, sliced thinly

1 small head iceberg lettuce

4 small skewers

BURGER SAUCE

2 tablespoons mayonnaise

2 tablespoons Sugar-Free Ketchup (page 251)

¼ teaspoon garlic powder

¼ teaspoon smoked paprika

STORAGE

Lettuce wrapped burgers are best fresh.

Refrigerate leftover burger patties (without toppings) for up to 4 days.

Unlock this recipe in the Easy Keto App

SOUPS & SANDWICHES

CREAMY CHICKEN ZOODLE SOUP

SERVING SIZE 1 cup | **SERVES 8**

When you're feeling under the weather or just craving comfort food on a cool day, nothing beats a warm bowl of chicken noodle soup. This version uses spiralized zucchini for the pasta and has a creamy broth base you're going to love.

1 tablespoon olive oil

½ large onion, diced

½ cup diced carrots

5 cups chicken broth

1 pound boneless skinless chicken breasts, cut into bite-size pieces

1 medium bay leaf

1 (14-ounce) can coconut cream

¾ teaspoon sea salt, or to taste

½ teaspoon black pepper, or to taste

½ cup green peas

2 medium zucchini, spiralized and trimmed to noodle length

STORAGE

Refrigerate for up to 5 days.

Freeze for up to 3 months.

1. In a Dutch oven over medium heat, heat the olive oil. Add the onion and carrots. Sauté for 5 to 10 minutes, until soft and slightly browned.

2. Add the chicken broth, chicken, and bay leaf. Increase heat to medium-high to bring to a boil, then reduce heat and simmer for 20 minutes.

3. Add the coconut cream and stir until smooth. Season with salt and pepper to taste.

4. Add peas and zucchini noodles. Simmer for 3 to 5 minutes, until zoodles are tender.

TIPS & VARIATIONS

• Even with the peas and carrots, this soup is keto friendly at 6g net carbs, despite these ingredients being typically avoided on a keto lifestyle, at least on their own. If you still prefer not to use the peas and carrots, replace them with diced celery and bell peppers. Add them with the onion rather than at the end.

• Tired of zoodles? Try spaghetti squash instead. Roast it first (instructions on page 23) before adding it to the soup.

• I used regular chicken broth, but bone broth works great as well. The amount of salt may need adjustment depending on the kind you use.

• If you are not dairy-free, you can use heavy cream instead of coconut cream. Heavy cream is a bit richer, so start with 1 cup and adjust to taste.

Unlock this recipe in the Easy Keto App
←

NUTRITION INFO: 260 Calories | 20.5g Fat | 8.4g Total Carbs | 2.4g Fiber | 6g Net Carbs | 13.2g Protein

TURKEY PESTO PANINI

SERVING SIZE 1 panini | **SERVES 2**

A panini is a warm, grilled Italian sandwich—and you don't need a panini press to make one! I make mine on a grill pan, but a regular skillet is just fine if that's all you have. This version uses my 90-Second Flax Bread so that it comes together fast, but feel free to swap in another bread recipe from the book, like Perfect Yeast Bread (page 49) or Rosemary Focaccia (page 45).

1. Slice the flax bread from both ramekins in half to make two slices each. Spread a thin layer of pesto sauce over all four pieces of bread.

2. Divide the sandwich fillings over the two pieces of bread in the following order: turkey, provolone, spinach, and sun-dried tomatoes. Top both sandwiches with a second piece of bread.

3. Heat the olive oil in a cast iron grill pan (or skillet) over medium-low heat, until shimmering but not smoking hot. Add the two sandwiches, cover with a lid, and cook for 2 to 3 minutes, until browned grill marks form on the bottom and cheese starts to melt.

4. Flip the paninis and place a smaller heavy skillet on top of the sandwiches, pressing down. Cook for 1 to 2 minutes, until browned grill marks form on the other side and cheese is melted.

1 doubled recipe (4 slices) 90-Second Flax Bread (page 46)

2 tablespoons pesto sauce

1½ ounces deli turkey slices

2 slices provolone cheese

5 grams (8 to 10 leaves) fresh spinach

1 tablespoon chopped sun-dried tomatoes

1 teaspoon olive oil

STORAGE

Refrigerate for up to 2 days.

Freeze for up to 3 months, if made without spinach.

TIPS & VARIATIONS

• Try these other panini flavor combos:
  ▸ **French Onion:** caramelized onions, Gruyere cheese, fresh thyme
  ▸ **Chicken Avocado:** mayonnaise, cooked chicken, sliced avocado, sliced tomatoes
  ▸ **Ham & Swiss:** Dijon mustard, deli ham slices, Swiss cheese
  ▸ **Veggie:** sliced tomatoes, sautéed mushrooms, spinach, Cheddar cheese
  ▸ **Strawberry Brie:** sliced strawberries, Brie cheese, fresh basil

• For a traditional square sandwich as shown here, make the flax bread in square ramekins instead of round ones.

NUTRITION INFO: 526 Calories | 45.1g Fat | 10.3g Total Carbs | 3.5g Fiber | 6.8g Net Carbs | 23.7g Protein

Unlock this recipe in the Easy Keto App

POTATO & RICE SUBSTITUTES

RUTABAGA FRIES

SERVING SIZE about 10 fries, or ⅛ of entire recipe | **SERVES 8**

Rutabagas are a less commonly known veggie, but they're one you should be familiar with if you love potatoes, because the texture is impeccably close. These keto fries are crispy on the outside, soft on the inside, just like a potato french fry! Plus, they are wonderfully simple to make. What's not to love?

3 pounds rutabagas

¼ cup avocado oil

1 teaspoon sea salt

¼ teaspoon black pepper

STORAGE

Fries are best fresh, as they lose their crispiness after reheating.

1. Preheat the oven to 400 degrees F.

2. Peel the rutabagas. Slice them into circles, ¼ inch thick. Stack the circles and slice them into sticks, between ¼ and ½ inch wide.

3. In a large bowl, toss the rutabaga sticks with avocado oil, salt, and pepper.

4. Place an oven-safe rack onto a large baking sheet. Arrange the fries in a single layer on the rack.

5. Bake for 35 to 45 minutes, until fries are soft on the inside and crispy on the outside.

TIPS & VARIATIONS

• Feel free to add your favorite french fry seasonings, such as garlic powder, onion powder, paprika, cayenne pepper, or even dried herbs. Or simply toss the fries with additional salt after baking.

• If you prefer, you can also deep-fry the rutabaga fries in avocado oil instead of baking in the oven.

Unlock this recipe in the Easy Keto App

NUTRITION INFO: 96 Calories | 7g Fat | 8.4g Total Carbs | 2.2g Fiber | 6.2g Net Carbs | 1g Protein

CILANTRO LIME CAULIFLOWER RICE

SERVING SIZE 1 cup | **SERVES 4**

Cilantro lime cauliflower rice is a low carb twist on a classic, bright, and flavorful rice dish. The combination of aromatic garlic, zesty lime, and fresh cilantro will ensure that your cauliflower rice is anything but boring. It pairs well alongside any Mexican entree or can be used as part of another recipe, such as Steak Burrito Bowls (page 132) or Mexican Beef & Rice Stuffed Peppers (page 143).

1. Heat olive oil in a large skillet over medium heat. Add the garlic and sauté for about 1 minute, until fragrant.

2. Add the cauliflower rice, lime zest, lime juice, salt, and pepper. Stir-fry for 3 to 5 minutes, until cauliflower rice is soft.

3. Remove from heat. Stir in the fresh cilantro.

3 tablespoons olive oil

2 cloves garlic, minced

1 pound (4 cups) cauliflower rice, fresh or frozen

½ medium lime, zested and juiced

1 teaspoon sea salt, or to taste

¼ teaspoon black pepper, or to taste

½ cup fresh cilantro, chopped

TIPS & VARIATIONS

• For a basic cauliflower rice without the cilantro-lime flavor, see the basic tutorial on page 17.

• If you like some heat, add crushed red pepper or cayenne pepper to taste.

STORAGE

Refrigerate for up to 5 days.

Freeze for 3 to 6 months.

NUTRITION INFO: 127 Calories | 10.9g Fat | 7.2g Total Carbs | 2.6g Fiber | 4.6g Net Carbs | 2.4g Protein

Unlock this recipe in the Easy Keto App

POTATO & RICE SUBSTITUTES

FAUX MASHED SWEET POTATOES

SERVING SIZE ½ cup | **SERVES 10**

While making a regular mashed potato swap is easy by substituting cauliflower (see Simple Mashed Cauliflower on page 77), finding a replacement for sweet potatoes is a bit trickier. In this recipe, we're using a combination of butternut squash and pumpkin to get the classic orange color and familiar autumn flavor, but you could use just one or the other as well. The addition of butter, cream, and Besti Brown sweetener make this dish as rich and sweet as the real thing.

1 head cauliflower, cut into florets

1 cup butternut squash, peeled and cut into ½-inch cubes

3 tablespoons olive oil

½ teaspoon sea salt, plus more to taste

¼ teaspoon black pepper

½ (15-ounce) can pumpkin puree, at room temperature, any liquid drained

1 tablespoon heavy cream

2 tablespoons butter, melted

1½ tablespoons Besti Brown Monk Fruit Allulose Blend, or to taste

STORAGE

Refrigerate for up to 5 days.

Freeze for 3 to 6 months.

1. Preheat the oven to 400 degrees F. Line 2 baking sheets with foil (grease lightly) or parchment paper.

2. In a large bowl, toss together the cauliflower florets, butternut squash, olive oil, salt, and pepper.

3. Arrange the vegetables in a single layer on the baking sheets. Roast in the oven for 25 to 30 minutes, rotating the pans halfway through, until fall-apart soft and golden.

4. Transfer the vegetables to a food processor. Add the pumpkin puree, heavy cream, and butter. Puree until smooth. Add Besti Brown and more salt to taste, then puree again.

TIPS & VARIATIONS

• I like to purchase pre-diced butternut squash from the produce section for convenience, but if that's not available, you can purchase one to peel and dice yourself. To get the 1 cup of cubed squash needed for this recipe, you'll need about half of a small (1½-pound) squash or quarter of a large (3-pound) squash.

• If you don't have both butternut squash and pumpkin, you can omit the pumpkin and add 1 extra cup of cubed squash, OR omit the squash and use the whole can (instead of ½ can) of the pumpkin puree. Carb count will vary slightly if you make these swaps.

• For a dairy-free version, replace the butter with your favorite dairy-free substitute, such as coconut oil, and swap the heavy cream with coconut cream.

Unlock this recipe in the Easy Keto App

NUTRITION INFO: 91 Calories | 7.2g Fat | 6.4g Total Carbs | 2.1g Fiber | 4.3g Net Carbs | 1.5g Protein

DIRTY CAULIFLOWER RICE

SERVING SIZE **1 cup** | SERVES 8

Dirty rice is a Creole dish that can easily be made keto friendly by swapping cauliflower rice for the white rice. It gets its brown color from being cooked with chicken liver, ground beef, and Cajun seasoning. Another bonus of using cauliflower rice here is that, unlike the original, it cooks very quickly—just 15 to 20 minutes from start to finish.

1. Heat 1 tablespoon of olive oil in a Dutch oven or large heavy-bottomed sauté pan over medium-high heat. Add the beef and chicken liver, and season with salt. Cook, breaking apart with a spatula, for 5 to 7 minutes, until browned.

2. Reduce heat to medium. Add the onion, bell pepper, celery, garlic, and Cajun seasoning. Cook, stirring occasionally, for 5 to 7 minutes, until onions are soft and translucent.

3. Add the cauliflower rice and chicken broth. Increase heat to bring to a simmer, then simmer for 3 to 5 minutes, until excess liquid is absorbed and cauliflower rice is soft. Stir in the remaining tablespoon of olive oil. Adjust salt to taste.

2 tablespoons olive oil, divided in half

8 ounces ground beef

8 ounces chicken liver, finely chopped

½ teaspoon sea salt, plus more to taste

½ large onion, diced

1 large bell pepper, diced

1 rib celery, diced

4 cloves garlic, minced

1 tablespoon Cajun seasoning

24 ounces (6 cups) cauliflower rice, fresh or frozen

½ cup chicken broth

STORAGE

Refrigerate for up to 5 days.

Freeze for 3 to 6 months.

TIPS & VARIATIONS

- To make livers easier to mince, freeze them for about 30 minutes first.

- If you're not a fan of liver, you can replace it with an additional 8 ounces of ground beef.

- I used the Cajun seasoning recipe from my Cajun seasoning recipe (**www.wholesomeyum.com/cajun-seasoning-mix-recipe**), which includes salt. If yours does not, adjust salt to taste after step 2.

- The serving size here makes a good main dish, but if you serve it as a side with something else, cut the serving size in half.

Unlock this recipe in the Easy Keto App

NUTRITION INFO: 386 Calories | 23.6g Fat | 15.4g Total Carbs | 5.4g Fiber | **10g Net Carbs** | 30.2g Protein

POTATO & RICE SUBSTITUTES

NUT FREE

VEGETARIAN OPTION

ZUCCHINI SKINS

SERVING SIZE 2 zucchini skins | **SERVES 4**

If you like loaded potato skins, these zucchini skins are the low carb equivalent. Hollowed out zucchini are stuffed with classically comforting toppings: smoky bacon, gooey cheese, tangy sour cream, and crisp green onions. Plus, I have three other variations for you to try on the opposite page. You won't even miss the potatoes!

2 medium zucchini

2 tablespoons olive oil

¼ teaspoon sea salt

¼ teaspoon black pepper

1 cup shredded Cheddar cheese

6 slices bacon, cooked and crumbled

⅓ cup sour cream

3 tablespoons sliced green onions

STORAGE

Refrigerate for up to 5 days.

Freeze for 3 to 6 months.

1. Preheat the oven to 400 degrees F.

2. Slice the zucchini in half lengthwise. Use a spoon or melon scoop to remove the seedy part of the zucchini flesh, creating a well in each zucchini half. Cut each zucchini half in half again, this time crosswise, for a total of 8 pieces.

3. Place the zucchini in a large baking dish, cut side up. Drizzle with olive oil. Sprinkle with salt and pepper. Bake for 5 minutes.

4. Remove the zucchini from the oven. Sprinkle each zucchini skin with about 2 tablespoons Cheddar and 2 teaspoons crumbled bacon.

5. Return zucchini to the oven for 5 to 10 minutes, until the cheese is melted and zucchini is tender. (Baking time will vary depending on the size of your zucchini.)

6. Top each zucchini with 2 teaspoons sour cream and 1 teaspoon green onions.

VARIATIONS

- **Spicy:** Sprinkle the zucchini with paprika and cayenne pepper in step 3.

- **Mexican:** Use Mexican cheese blend, bacon, and black olives in step 4. Finish with sour cream, salsa, and cilantro.

- **Mediterranean (vegetarian option):** Use Parmesan, black olives, red onions, and diced tomatoes in step 4. Finish with fresh basil.

- **Italian (vegetarian option):** Use marinara sauce, mozzarella, and Italian seasoning in step 4. Finish with fresh basil.

Unlock this recipe in the Easy Keto App

←

NUTRITION INFO: 368 Calories | 33.6g Fat | 4.8g Total Carbs | 1.1g Fiber | 3.7g Net Carbs | 12.9g Protein

TIPS & VARIATIONS

- For the smoothest cauliflower mash, use just the florets and as little of the stems as possible. The stems don't get as smooth as the florets.

- Make sure the cauliflower is cooked until it is super soft before pureeing. This will ensure a silky smooth mash.

- If you have a pound of riced cauliflower on hand, you can use that instead of florets. The method is the same, but the cook time will be shorter.

- For a dairy-free version, replace butter with olive oil and use a dairy-free cream cheese substitute.

SIMPLE MASHED CAULIFLOWER

SERVING SIZE ½ cup | **SERVES 4**

This mashed cauliflower is smooth, creamy, and buttery, just like real mashed potatoes should be. It's the perfect side dish for steak, chicken, or even fish. Be sure to follow my tips to get the smoothest texture.

OPTION 1: MICROWAVE METHOD

1. Place the cauliflower florets into a large bowl with ½ cup water. Cover the top with plastic wrap.

2. Microwave for 10 to 15 minutes, until very soft and mushy. Be careful removing the plastic wrap, as hot steam will escape. Drain and pat dry. Set aside.

OPTION 2: STEAM METHOD

1. Fill a large saucepan or pot with salted water and fit with a steamer basket. (The water should come up to just below the bottom of the basket.) Bring the water to a boil.

2. Place the cauliflower florets into the steamer basket and fit on top of the pan. Cover the pot.

3. Reduce water to a simmer and cook, covered, for 10 to 15 minutes, until cauliflower is very soft and mushy. Drain and pat dry. Set aside.

MAKE THE MASHED CAULIFLOWER

1. Heat olive oil in a small skillet over medium heat. Add the garlic and sauté for about 1 minute, until fragrant.

2. Place the cooked cauliflower, sautéed garlic, butter, cream cheese, and salt in a food processor. Puree for 1 to 2 minutes, until completely smooth. Adjust salt to taste.

1 large head cauliflower (6 cups florets)

1 teaspoon olive oil

2 cloves garlic, minced

2 tablespoons butter, cut into chunks

2 tablespoons cream cheese, cut into chunks

¾ teaspoon sea salt, or to taste

STORAGE

Refrigerate for up to 5 days.

Freeze for 3 to 6 months.

Unlock this recipe in the Easy Keto App

NUTRITION INFO: 132 Calories | 9.6g Fat | 9.9g Total Carbs | 3.8g Fiber | 6.1g Net Carbs | 4g Protein

POTATO & RICE SUBSTITUTES

77

LEMON GARLIC ASPARAGUS RISOTTO

SERVING SIZE 1 cup | **SERVES 4**

Risotto is an Italian dish that combines short-grain rice with a rich, creamy sauce. This cauliflower rice version features a garlicky, lemon-infused sauce and asparagus to make it light and bright.

2 tablespoons butter

¼ large onion, diced

8 ounces asparagus, trimmed, cut into 1-inch pieces

3 cloves garlic, minced

1 pound (4 cups) cauliflower rice, fresh or frozen

½ cup chicken broth

¾ cup heavy cream

⅓ cup grated Parmesan cheese

1 tablespoon lemon zest

½ teaspoon sea salt, or to taste

¼ teaspoon black pepper, or to taste

STORAGE

Refrigerate for up to 5 days.

Freeze for 3 to 6 months.

1. In a sauté pan over medium heat, melt the butter. Add the onions and sauté for about 8 to 10 minutes, until onions are translucent and starting to brown.

2. Add the asparagus and sauté for 2 to 3 minutes, until starting to turn bright green but still crisp-tender and not quite done.

3. Add the garlic. Sauté for about 1 minute, until fragrant.

4. Add the cauliflower rice and chicken broth. Increase heat to bring to a boil, then simmer, stirring occasionally, until the cauliflower rice is tender and liquid is slightly reduced, about 3 to 4 minutes.

5. Reduce heat to low. Stir in the heavy cream, Parmesan, and lemon zest. Continue to heat, stirring constantly, for about 1 minute, until the cheese melts and the sauce is smooth. Season with salt and pepper to taste.

TIPS & VARIATIONS

• Lemon zest provides the best lemon flavor, but if you prefer you can use 2 to 3 teaspoons of lemon juice instead.

• If you want a more basic risotto, omit the asparagus; the lemon zest is optional.

• For a vegetarian version, swap the chicken broth with vegetable broth.

Unlock this recipe in the Easy Keto App

NUTRITION INFO: 288 Calories | 24.7g Fat | 11.4g Total Carbs | 3.9g Fiber | 7.5g Net Carbs | 8.3g Protein

TIPS & VARIATIONS

- The sauce thickens rapidly when it cools, so if it has cooled down while you were arranging the radishes, reheat gently over low heat, until smooth and slightly runny. If it cooks down too much, you can thin it out with more broth or cream.

- If you don't like radishes, you can make the same dish with other low carb root vegetables, such as turnips, jicama, or rutabagas, or use roasted cauliflower.

- For a vegetarian version, swap the chicken broth with vegetable broth.

SCALLOPED RADISHES

SERVING SIZE ½ cup | **SERVES 8**

Scalloped radishes are a low carb twist on scalloped potatoes. While traditional scalloped potato recipes bake the raw potatoes in sauce, we don't have a flour thickener here like they do, so we precook the radishes and then assemble and bake briefly. Roasting the radish slices removes the bite and leaves them mild and starchy. The final is the same creamy, cheesy goodness you expect from scalloped potatoes, minus the carbs.

1. Preheat the oven to 400 degrees F.

2. In a large bowl, toss the sliced radishes in olive oil. Arrange them in a single layer on a large baking sheet. Sprinkle lightly with salt.

3. Roast radish slices for about 15 minutes, until soft.

4. Melt the butter in a large skillet over medium heat. Add the onion and sauté for about 5 minutes, until translucent.

5. Add the garlic and sauté for about 1 minute, until fragrant.

6. Reduce heat to low. Stir in the chicken broth and heavy cream. Gradually add 1½ cups of Cheddar cheese, stirring constantly, until a smooth sauce forms. Season with pepper. Turn off heat and cover the pan to keep warm.

7. Arrange half of the radish slices in overlapping rows in a 9 x 9-inch baking dish. Pour half of the cheese sauce over the radishes. Repeat with a second layer of radishes and cheese sauce. Sprinkle the remaining ½ cup of Cheddar on top.

8. Bake for about 5 minutes, until the cheese on top is melted.

1½ pounds trimmed radishes, sliced into ⅛-inch-thick rounds

1 tablespoon olive oil

¼ teaspoon sea salt

2 tablespoons butter

½ small onion, diced

4 cloves garlic, minced

½ cup chicken broth

½ cup heavy cream

2 cups shredded Cheddar cheese, divided (1½ cups and ½ cup)

¼ teaspoon black pepper

STORAGE

Scalloped radishes are best fresh; sauce may separate when reheating.

NUTRITION INFO: 224 Calories | 19.5g Fat | 4.6g Total Carbs | 1.5g Fiber | **3.1g Net Carbs** | 8.3g Protein

Unlock this recipe in the Easy Keto App

POTATO & RICE SUBSTITUTES

NUT FREE

VEGETARIAN OPTION

LOADED JUST-LIKE-POTATO SALAD

SERVING SIZE ½ cup | **SERVES 5**

This creamy salad is like a cross between potato salad and loaded baked potatoes. Cooked celery root has a neutral flavor and texture that is very close to that of white potatoes, making it the perfect stand-in for this recipe.

4 slices bacon

12 ounces (2 to 2½ cups) peeled celery root, cut into ½-inch cubes

3 tablespoons mayonnaise

3 tablespoons sour cream

½ teaspoon Dijon mustard

¼ teaspoon garlic powder

¼ teaspoon sea salt

⅛ teaspoon black pepper

⅓ cup shredded Cheddar cheese

2 tablespoons sliced green onions

STORAGE

Refrigerate for up to 5 days.

1. Place the bacon into a large, cold skillet in a single layer. (Work in batches if it doesn't all fit.) Place the skillet over medium heat and fry for 10 to 15 minutes, turning every few minutes, until browned and crispy. Chop the bacon into small pieces. Set aside to cool.

2. Meanwhile, place celery root into a pot and cover with water. Bring to a boil over high heat, then reduce to medium and simmer for about 15 minutes, until soft and tender. Drain, run under cool water, and pat dry.

3. In a medium bowl, whisk together the mayonnaise, sour cream, mustard, garlic powder, salt, and pepper.

4. Fold in the celery root, chopped bacon, Cheddar, and green onions.

TIPS & VARIATIONS

• To get 12 ounces peeled celery root, you'll need about 1 pound unpeeled root, not including greens.

• Celery root is sometimes called celeriac at the grocery store; it looks like a bumpy beige root vegetable about the size of a softball, with a leafy top that looks like parsley. You can also substitute rutabagas, turnips, radishes, or cauliflower, but the cook time will vary.

• You can serve the salad immediately, but for the best flavor, chill for 2 hours before serving.

• For a vegetarian version, omit the bacon.

Unlock this recipe in the Easy Keto App

←

NUTRITION INFO: 260 Calories | 22.2g Fat | 8.9g Total Carbs | 1.7g Fiber | 7.2g Net Carbs | 6.7g Protein

TIPS & VARIATIONS

- There are many variations of paella. I kept this one as simple as possible, with 10 mandatory ingredients and a few optional. If you like, feel free to add chicken (add at the same time as the chorizo) or your favorite seafood, such as mussels, clams or even lobster (add at the same time as the shrimp).

- Although saffron is expensive, it's a crucial ingredient in paella. Ethnic markets often have it at more reasonable prices than the grocery store. You can substitute turmeric to achieve the same yellow color, but the flavor will be very different.

- To add even more golden color to your paella, add a teaspoon of turmeric at the same time as the salt and pepper.

PAELLA

SERVING SIZE 1½ cups | SERVES 6

When my husband and I took a trip to Spain a few years ago, paella was everywhere, from the fanciest restaurants to the most casual fast food joints. It was common to see a couple dozen ingredients in their dishes, but to keep this recipe simple, I pulled out the key components that I saw over and over. Of course, we are swapping the ubiquitous rice with cauliflower rice for a healthy low carb version.

1. In a small bowl (or saucepan), heat the chicken broth in the microwave (or on the stove), until hot. Remove from heat. Crumble the saffron threads into the broth, stir, and set aside.

2. Heat the olive oil in a paella pan (or large sauté pan) over medium-high heat. Add the onion and bell pepper. Sauté for 5 to 6 minutes, until onions are translucent and peppers are soft.

3. Add the garlic. Sauté for 1 to 2 minutes, until fragrant.

4. Add the chorizo. Sauté for 5 to 6 minutes, until hot and cooked through.

5. Add the diced tomatoes, saffron broth, smoked paprika (if using), and cauliflower rice. Season with salt and pepper. Stir together, then nestle the shrimp in the cauliflower rice.

6. Increase heat to bring the broth to a boil. Cover and simmer for 3 to 5 minutes, until cauliflower and shrimp are both cooked through.

7. If desired, garnish with chopped parsley and a squeeze of lemon.

¾ cup chicken broth

6 saffron threads

2 tablespoons olive oil

½ large onion, diced

1 large red bell pepper, diced

4 cloves garlic, minced

1 pound chorizo, removed from casings and crumbled

1 (14½-ounce) can diced tomatoes, drained

1 teaspoon smoked paprika, optional

24 ounces (6 cups) cauliflower rice, fresh or frozen

½ teaspoon sea salt

¼ teaspoon black pepper

12 ounces large shrimp, peeled and deveined

Chopped parsley, for garnish, optional

Lemon wedges, for garnish, optional

STORAGE

Refrigerate for up to 5 days.

Freeze for 3 to 6 months.

POTATO & RICE SUBSTITUTES

Unlock this recipe in the Easy Keto App

NUTRITION INFO: 395 Calories | 24.9g Fat | 16.1g Total Carbs | 3.8g Fiber | 12.3g Net Carbs | 25.4g Protein

CRISPY BAKED CAULIFLOWER TOTS

SERVING SIZE 6 tots | **SERVES 4**

Tater tots should be crispy on the outside and soft on the inside, and that's exactly what you get with these baked cauliflower tots. The small amount of coconut flour works to absorb the moisture in the cauliflower, while the pork rind coating creates the crisp exterior.

1 tablespoon avocado oil (for frying, plus more for greasing baking sheet)

12 ounces (3 cups) cauliflower rice, fresh or frozen

⅛ teaspoon sea salt

1 large egg

1 large egg white

⅓ cup shredded mozzarella cheese

⅓ cup grated Parmesan cheese

1 tablespoon coconut flour

1½ ounces pork rinds, crushed in a blender (makes ¾ cup)

Sugar-Free Ketchup, optional (page 251)

STORAGE

Refrigerate for up to 5 days.

Reheat in a skillet to crisp up.

Freeze for 3 to 6 months.

1. Preheat the oven to 375 degrees F. Line a baking sheet with parchment paper and grease lightly.

2. Heat the avocado oil in a large sauté pan or wok over medium-high heat. Add the cauliflower rice and season with salt. Stir-fry for 3 to 5 minutes, until the cauliflower is very soft and lightly browned, with no moisture left in the pan. (It's important that all the moisture cooks away, or your tots will fall apart.)

3. Meanwhile, whisk the egg and egg white in a large bowl. Stir in the mozzarella, Parmesan, and coconut flour.

4. When the cauliflower rice is done, add it to the bowl and stir to combine.

5. Place crushed pork rinds into a bowl. Use a small cookie scoop to pick up balls of the "dough." Form small tater tot–size cylinders (about 1 inch long and ¾ inch wide), roll in crushed pork rinds, and place on the baking sheet.

6. Bake for 15 to 20 minutes, flipping halfway through, until golden. Serve with Sugar-Free Ketchup (page 251).

TIPS & VARIATIONS

- The pork rinds help the tots get a crispy exterior. If you don't like or eat them, or want a vegetarian option, you can skip this coating. I don't recommend using a different breading, such as almond flour, as it won't get crispy with this recipe.

- You can also fry the tots in olive or avocado oil over medium heat, instead of baking.

Unlock this recipe in the Easy Keto App

NUTRITION INFO: 165 Calories | 10.6g Fat | 5.9g Total Carbs | 2.4g Fiber | 3.5g Net Carbs | 12.1g Protein

|PIZZA

TIPS & VARIATIONS

- You can use raw ground chicken instead of shredded chicken if you prefer. Unlike the shredded chicken, ground chicken does not need to be precooked. The crust bake time will be about 20 to 22 minutes.

- The crust texture is best when using a pizza stone, but if you don't have one, you can bake the crust on a pizza pan or baking sheet. Just make sure you still use parchment paper when you parbake it; otherwise, the crust will stick easily.

- As with any pizza, feel free to customize this one with any sauce and toppings you like. Chicken pizza crust pairs particularly well with white sauce, but you can also use sugar-free marinara sauce.

CHICKEN CRUST PIZZA

SERVING SIZE 2 slices, or ¼ entire pizza | SERVES 4

Pizza crust made out of chicken may sound like an unusual combination, but try it and you'll be convinced. Unlike most keto pizzas, this one doesn't require any low carb flours or specialty ingredients; instead, it needs just four common ingredients (plus salt) that you probably often have on hand. The best part is, it's easy to customize to your liking!

1. Preheat the oven to 400 degrees F, with a pizza stone inside. Line a pizza peel with parchment paper.

2. In a large bowl, stir together the chicken, Parmesan, garlic, and salt.

3. In a separate bowl, whisk the eggs lightly, then add to the large bowl. Mix well.

4. Spread the chicken crust pizza "dough" into a circle, about ¼-inch thick, on the parchment-lined pizza peel.

5. Slide the dough with the parchment paper onto the pizza stone in the oven. Bake for 15 to 20 minutes, until firm and golden around the edges.

6. To remove the crust from the oven, slide the pizza peel underneath the parchment paper leaving the pizza stone inside. Let the crust rest for 10 minutes, which helps to "seal" it so that it won't get soggy from the sauce.

7. Add sauce, spinach, red onion, and mozzarella, in that order. Use the pizza peel to return the pizza to the oven, directly onto the pizza stone without parchment, for 10 to 15 minutes, until the cheese is melted. If desired, place under the broiler for 1 to 3 minutes to brown the cheese.

CHICKEN CRUST

¾ pound cooked chicken, shredded (cooked weight; equivalent to 1 pound raw)

½ cup grated Parmesan cheese

2 cloves garlic, minced

½ teaspoon sea salt

2 large eggs

TOPPINGS

½ cup Alfredo Sauce (page 248)

¾ cup packed spinach

⅓ cup red onion, sliced thin into half moons

1 cup shredded mozzarella cheese

STORAGE

Refrigerate for up to 5 days.

Freeze for 3 to 6 months.

NUT FREE

NUTRITION INFO: 433 Calories | 29.2g Fat | 4.7g Total Carbs | 0.4g Fiber | 4.3g Net Carbs | 35.8g Protein

Unlock this recipe in the Easy Keto App

PIZZA

STUFFED-CRUST DEEP-DISH PIZZA

SERVING SIZE 1 slice of pizza, or ⅛ entire recipe | **SERVES 8**

This deep-dish pizza is based on my most popular fathead pizza recipe, transformed into a deep-dish crust, with cheese stuffed into the crust edges. The taste and texture is impeccably close to a real deep-dish pizza! My complete guide to fathead dough can be found in my first book, The Easy Keto Cookbook, *but you can find the condensed version in this book on page 15.*

DOUGH

1½ cups super fine blanched almond flour

2 large eggs

2½ cups shredded mozzarella cheese

2 ounces cream cheese, cut into cubes

4 whole mozzarella string cheese sticks, cut in half crosswise

TOPPINGS

¾ cup marinara sauce

1 cup shredded mozzarella cheese

1½ ounces cooked Italian sausage

1 ounce pepperoni slices

STORAGE

Refrigerate for up to 5 days.

Freeze for 3 to 6 months.

1. Preheat the oven to 425 degrees F. Grease a 9-inch springform pan with cooking spray, butter, or coconut oil.

2. In a food processor, process the almond flour and eggs, until smooth.

3. In a large bowl, microwave the mozzarella and cream cheese for about 90 seconds, or heat in a double boiler on the stove, stirring halfway through, until smooth.

4. Add the cheese to the food processor, positioning the cheese so that the blades are sticking into it, and process until a dough forms. Pulse or scrape the sides as necessary.

5. Form the dough into a ball. If it's sticky, cover with plastic and refrigerate for 30 minutes, or until no longer sticky. Press the dough into the bottom of the springform pan, going up the sides about 1½ inches.

6. Arrange the halved mozzarella cheese sticks along the edge of the crust in the pan and fold the edges of the dough to cover the cheese, pressing to seal.

7. Using a fork or toothpick, poke holes all over the bottom of the crust to prevent bubbling. (Do not poke the stuffed crust edges.)

8. Bake the crust for 6 minutes. Remove from the oven and poke the bottom all over with a fork to deflate any bubbles. Return to the oven and bake for 5 to 7 minutes, until golden brown.

9. Layer the toppings on the crust in the following order: marinara sauce, mozzarella, Italian sausage, and pepperoni. Bake for an additional 8 to 10 minutes, until the cheese is melted.

NUTRITION INFO: 377 Calories | 28.8g Fat | 8.5g Total Carbs | 2.7g Fiber | 5.8g Net Carbs | 23.6g Protein

Unlock this recipe in the Easy Keto App

TIPS & VARIATIONS

- If you want to lower carbs further, swap the marinara sauce with Alfredo Sauce (page 248).

- The toppings are completely customizable to your liking. Be sure any meats you add are precooked. Make it vegetarian by topping with low carb veggies instead, like mushrooms (sauté them a bit first) and bell peppers.

- The number of mozzarella sticks you need might vary depending on the brand; use enough to go all the way around the crust edge.

CLOUD VEGGIE PIZZAS

SERVING SIZE 2 mini pizzas | SERVES 6

These veggie pizzas use simple cloud bread as the crust, making them super light on both carbs and calories. They make a quick, easy, and delicious vegetarian meal—or pile them high with meat toppings if that's your thing.

1. Make 12 servings of cloud bread according to the instructions on page 41. Cool to room temperature.

2. While cloud bread is cooling, preheat the oven to 400 degrees F.

3. Arrange mushrooms in a single layer on a small baking sheet and drizzle with olive oil. Roast in the oven for 12 to 15 minutes, until mushrooms are tender.

4. Arrange the cooled cloud bread on a large baking sheet.

5. Spread 2 teaspoons of marinara sauce on each piece of cloud bread. Sprinkle with mozzarella. Top with bell peppers, black olives, and roasted mushrooms.

6. Bake for about 10 minutes, until the cheese is melted.

1 doubled recipe (12 pieces) Dairy-Free Cloud Bread (page 41)

1½ cups sliced mushrooms

2 teaspoons olive oil

½ cup marinara sauce

¾ cup shredded mozzarella cheese

¾ cup diced bell peppers

⅓ cup sliced black olives

STORAGE

Refrigerate for up to 5 days.
Freeze for 3 to 6 months.

TIPS & VARIATIONS

- Feel free to customize toppings to your liking. Try meat lover's with sausage and pepperoni, or white pizza using the same toppings from the Chicken Crust Pizza recipe on page 91.

- For a lower carb option, replace the marinara sauce with Alfredo Sauce (page 248).

- For a dairy-free version, simply omit the cheese.

- If you like the colorful presentation shown here, use bell peppers in different colors.

NUTRITION INFO: 303 Calories | 25.8g Fat | 6.9g Total Carbs | 2.5g Fiber | **4.4g Net Carbs** | 12.4g Protein

Unlock this recipe in the Easy Keto App

PEPPERONI PIZZA CUPS

SERVING SIZE 2 cups | **SERVES 12**

Pepperoni pizza cups are like mini savory pie crusts filled with pizza sauce and toppings. They make a fun appetizer that can feed a crowd, or meal prep the recipe ahead of time to enjoy either as a quick snack or lunch paired with a green salad.

DOUGH

2½ cups super fine blanched almond flour

2 tablespoons golden flaxseed meal

2 teaspoons Italian seasoning

1 teaspoon garlic powder

½ teaspoon sea salt

3 tablespoons butter, melted

2 large eggs, whisked

FILLING

1 cup marinara sauce

1½ cups shredded mozzarella cheese

2 ounces mini pepperoni slices

STORAGE

Refrigerate for up to 5 days.

Freeze for 3 to 6 months.

1. Preheat the oven to 350 degrees F. Line 24 cups in a mini muffin tin with parchment paper liners.

2. In a large bowl, mix together the almond flour, flaxseed meal, Italian seasoning, garlic powder, and salt.

3. Stir in the melted butter, then the eggs, until a dense, uniform, slightly crumbly dough forms.

4. Press the dough into the lined muffin cups, going up the sides, using about 1 tablespoon of dough per cup. Crusts should be thin, about ¼ inch thick.

5. Bake for about 10 minutes, until semi-firm but not quite golden. Remove from oven, but leave the oven on at 350 degrees F. Cool pizza cups for about 15 minutes, until warm but no longer hot.

6. Fill each cup with 2 teaspoons marinara sauce, sprinkle with 1 tablespoon mozzarella, and top with 4 mini pepperoni slices.

7. Bake for 10 minutes, until the cheese is melted. If desired, place under the broiler for 1 to 2 minutes to brown the cheese.

TIPS & VARIATIONS

• The easiest way to press the crusts into the cups is to use a small cookie scoop to pack the dough, release onto your hand, flatten with your palm into a thin disk, then press into the lined pan.

• A serving of 2 cups is perfect for an appetizer. If you want to serve these cups as a meal, double the serving size.

• For a dairy-free version, replace the butter in the crust with coconut oil and omit the cheese on top.

Unlock this recipe in the Easy Keto App

NUTRITION INFO: 249 Calories | 20.7g Fat | 7.7g Total Carbs | 3.3g Fiber | **4.4g Net Carbs** | 11.2g Protein

PROSCIUTTO FLATBREAD

SERVING SIZE 1 slice, or ⅛ entire recipe | **SERVES 8**

If you get bored with classic pizza sauce and toppings (is that even possible?!), make prosciutto flatbread instead. It features a seasoned, garlicky crust topped with olive oil, thin prosciutto, creamy goat cheese, sweet red onions, and fresh arugula leaves. It's yummy as an appetizer, or double the serving size for a full meal.

DOUGH

⅓ cup coconut flour

2 large eggs

1 teaspoon Italian seasoning

1 teaspoon garlic powder, optional

¼ teaspoon sea salt

1½ cups shredded mozzarella cheese

1 ounce cream cheese, cubed

TOPPINGS

4 tablespoons extra-virgin olive oil, divided (1 tablespoon, 2 tablespoons, and 1 tablespoon)

½ medium red onion, sliced into thin quarter moons

2 ounces thin prosciutto slices, cut into large pieces

2 ounces crumbled goat cheese

1 cup packed arugula

STORAGE

Refrigerate for up to 5 days.

Freeze for 3 to 6 months.

1. Preheat the oven to 400 degrees F, with a pizza stone inside.

2. In a food processor, blend the coconut flour, eggs, Italian seasoning, garlic powder (if using), and salt, until smooth.

3. Combine the mozzarella and cream cheese in a large bowl. Microwave for 90 seconds, stirring halfway through, then stir again until smooth.

4. Add the cheese to the food processor, positioning the cheese so that the blades are sticking into it, and process until a dough forms. Pulse or scrape the sides as necessary. Form the dough into a ball. If it's sticky, cover with plastic and refrigerate for 30 minutes.

5. Place the dough between 2 pieces of lightly oiled parchment paper and roll out into an oval shape, ¼ inch thick.

6. Lift the top piece of parchment paper. Poke holes in the top of the crust with a fork. Slide the crust and bottom piece of parchment together onto a pizza peel, then slide the crust and parchment onto the pizza stone in the oven. Bake for 7 to 8 minutes, until just barely golden around the edges but not dark. If it puffs up, poke with a fork and let it deflate.

7. Meanwhile, heat 1 tablespoon of the olive oil in a large skillet over medium heat. Add the red onions and sauté for about 5 minutes, until soft and translucent.

8. When the crust is done, remove it from the oven, leaving the pizza stone inside and the oven on. Brush 2 tablespoons of the olive oil over the crust, leaving a ½-inch border around the edges. Top with red onions, prosciutto, and goat cheese.

Unlock this recipe in the Easy Keto App

NUTRITION INFO: 259 Calories | 19.2g Fat | 10.1g Total Carbs | 6.3g Fiber | 3.8g Net Carbs | 11.4g Protein

TIPS & VARIATIONS

- **Caprese topping (vegetarian):** tomatoes, fresh basil, fresh mozzarella, and sugar-free balsamic glaze

- **Kale Parmesan topping (vegetarian):** sautéed kale, shaved Parmesan, minced garlic, and pine nuts

- **Jalapeno Bacon topping:** cream cheese, sliced jalapenos, crumbled bacon, and fresh cilantro

- The crust texture is best when using a pizza stone, but if you don't have one, you can bake it on a pizza pan as well. Just make sure you still use parchment paper when you parbake the crust, because it will stick easily otherwise.

9. Slide the flatbread directly onto the pizza stone in the oven (without parchment paper this time) and bake for 5 to 8 minutes, until the toppings are hot.

10. Remove flatbread from the oven and top with arugula. Drizzle with the remaining tablespoon of olive oil.

PIZZA

TIPS & VARIATIONS

- If the dough is too sticky to work with even after chilling, oil your hands and the parchment paper to make it easier.

- If you prefer a more traditional pizza filling, swap the Alfredo Sauce with marinara and replace the spinach and tomatoes with pepperoni and/or precooked sausage.

WHITE PIZZA POCKETS

SERVING SIZE 1 pizza pocket | SERVES 6

White pizza pockets are like a personal-size calzone that tastes like pure comfort food: soft and chewy dough filled with a creamy, cheesy filling. My top reason for making these pockets? Meal prep! They freeze surprisingly well and are delicious reheated for a quick lunch.

1. Preheat the oven to 350 degrees F. Line a baking sheet with parchment paper.

2. In a food processor, process the almond flour and eggs, until smooth.

3. Combine the mozzarella and cream cheese in a large bowl. Microwave for 90 seconds, or heat in a double boiler on the stove, stirring halfway through, then stir again until smooth.

4. Add the cheese to the food processor, positioning the cheese so that the blades are sticking into it, and process until a dough forms. Pulse or scrape the sides as necessary.

5. Form the dough into a ball, cover with plastic, and chill for 30 minutes, until no longer sticky. (Sometimes you can skip this step with fathead dough, but this recipe requires folding and shaping, so it's best to chill.)

6. Meanwhile, make the filling. In a large bowl, stir together the Alfredo Sauce, spinach, tomatoes, and mozzarella.

7. Place the ball of dough between 2 pieces of greased or lightly oiled parchment paper and roll into a large, thin rectangle, ¼ inch thick. Remove the top piece of parchment and cut the rectangle into 6 squares. Place ⅙ of the filling onto half of one square, leaving a ½-inch border. Fold over the other half of the dough to form a rectangular pocket and seal the edges. Repeat with the remaining dough and filling, making 6 pockets total. Place the pockets onto the prepared baking sheet.

8. Bake for about 20 minutes, until the pockets are golden brown.

DOUGH

1½ cups super fine blanched almond flour

2 large eggs

3 cups shredded mozzarella cheese

2 ounces cream cheese, cubed

FILLING

¾ cup Alfredo Sauce (page 248)

3 ounces frozen spinach, drained and squeezed

2 medium roma tomatoes, seeded and chopped

⅔ cup shredded mozzarella cheese

STORAGE

Refrigerate for up to 5 days.

Freeze for 3 to 6 months.

NUTRITION INFO: 556 Calories | 46.8g Fat | 10.9g Total Carbs | 3.7g Fiber | 7.2g Net Carbs | 25.9g Protein

Unlock this recipe in the Easy Keto App

PIZZA

PEPPERONI PIZZA ROLLS

SERVING SIZE 2 pizza rolls | **SERVES 6**

I grew up eating pizza rolls from the freezer section, but who knows why they were called pizza rolls, as they were more like little pockets. This version has a true roll shape instead—and is made without all the carbs and processed ingredients. It is filling and chewy, and makes a fun snack or meal.

DOUGH

1½ cups super fine blanched almond flour

2 large eggs

1 teaspoon baking powder

¼ teaspoon xanthan gum, optional

2½ cups shredded mozzarella cheese

2 ounces cream cheese, cubed

FILLING

½ cup marinara sauce

½ tablespoon Italian seasoning

2 cups shredded mozzarella cheese

4 ounces pepperoni slices

TOPPING

¼ cup shredded mozzarella cheese

STORAGE

Refrigerate for up to 5 days.
Freeze for 3 to 6 months.

Unlock this recipe in the Easy Keto App

1. In a food processor, blend the almond flour, eggs, baking powder, and xanthan gum (if using), until smooth.

2. Combine the mozzarella and cream cheese in a large bowl. Microwave for 90 seconds, stirring halfway through, then stir again until smooth.

3. Add the cheese to the food processor, positioning the cheese so that the blades are sticking into it, and process until a dough forms. Pulse or scrape the sides as necessary.

4. Form the dough into a ball. If it's sticky, cover with plastic and refrigerate for about 30 minutes, until no longer sticky.

5. Place the ball of dough between 2 pieces of lightly oiled parchment paper and roll out into a very thin rectangle, about ⅛ inch thick, 15 inches long, and 12 inches wide.

6. Spread marinara sauce over the rectangle, leaving a ½-inch border with no sauce. Sprinkle with Italian seasoning, then mozzarella. Top with pepperoni.

7. Starting from the short side and using the parchment paper to help you, roll the rectangle tightly into a log, peeling away the parchment paper as you go.

8. Place the log in the freezer for 30 minutes. (This will help it stay together when slicing the pizza rolls.)

9. Meanwhile, preheat the oven to 375 degrees F. Line a baking sheet with parchment paper.

10. Remove the log from the freezer and use a sharp knife to slice crosswise, forming 12 pinwheels, 1 inch thick.

11. Place pinwheels onto the prepared baking sheet at least 1 inch apart, spirals facing up. Sprinkle a teaspoon of mozzarella on top of each.

12. Bake for about 20 minutes, until the rolls are golden brown.

NUTRITION INFO: 540 Calories | 41.2g Fat | 11.1g Total Carbs | 3.7g Fiber | 7.4g Net Carbs | 34.2g Protein

PIZZA

PASTA

NUT FREE OPTION

VEGETARIAN

CAULIFLOWER MAC & CHEESE

SERVING SIZE 1 cup | **SERVES 4**

Cauliflower mac and cheese has the same creamy, cheesy sauce you love in real mac and cheese, but swaps the pasta for roasted cauliflower. (Make sure your florets are small for a feeling reminiscent of the classic elbow macaroni!) The sauce really shines here, so this dish a great way to sneak in a veggie without it being the main focus.

1 head cauliflower, cut into small florets

2 tablespoons olive oil

½ teaspoon sea salt

¼ teaspoon black pepper

1 cup shredded Cheddar cheese

¼ cup heavy cream

¼ cup unsweetened almond milk

1 tablespoon butter

STORAGE

Refrigerate for up to 4 days.
Freeze for 3 months.

1. Preheat the oven to 450 degrees F. Line a baking sheet with foil or parchment paper.

2. In a large bowl, toss the cauliflower florets, olive oil, salt, and pepper.

3. Arrange the cauliflower florets on the prepared baking sheet. Roast for about 15 to 20 minutes, until tender.

4. In a small saucepan over low heat, heat the Cheddar cheese, heavy cream, almond milk, and butter, stirring frequently, until smooth. Be careful not to overheat.

5. When the cauliflower is done, transfer it to a large bowl. Pour the cheese sauce over the cauliflower and gently fold the sauce into the cauliflower until coated evenly.

TIPS & VARIATIONS

• If you like mac and cheese with a crumb topping, transfer the mixture to a baking dish after the last step, sprinkle with crushed pork rinds, and broil for a few minutes until golden.

• The sauce can be made with any cheese you like that melts well. Try Gruyere or Gouda if you like stronger flavors.

• For a nut-free version, substitute coconut milk beverage (or simply more cream) for the almond milk.

Unlock this recipe in the Easy Keto App
←

NUTRITION INFO: 279 Calories | 23.9g Fat | 8.1g Total Carbs | 3.1g Fiber | 5g Net Carbs | 10.4g Protein

SPAGHETTI SQUASH ALFREDO

SERVING SIZE **1 cup** | SERVES 4

NUT FREE

VEGETARIAN

Spaghetti squash noodles might not have an identical shape and texture to classic fettuccine, but when you smother them in creamy alfredo sauce, it feels pretty close. You get the same sensation of twirling noodles around a fork, at a fraction of the carbs.

1. Preheat the oven to 425 degrees F. Line a baking sheet with foil and grease lightly.

2. Slice the spaghetti squash in half. To make it easier, score where you're planning to cut first. Scoop out the seeds.

3. Place the spaghetti squash halves onto the baking sheet, cut side up. Drizzle with olive oil, then sprinkle with salt and pepper. Flip the pieces over, cut side down.

4. Roast spaghetti squash for 25 to 35 minutes, until a knife can easily pierce the skin with very little resistance.

5. Meanwhile, make the Alfredo Sauce. (See instructions on 248.)

6. Remove the squash from the oven and let rest for 10 minutes. Use a fork to scrape the squash from the shells, with the tines perpendicular to the length of the squash, and release the strands.

7. Transfer the spaghetti squash noodles to a large bowl. Add the sauce and toss to coat. Sprinkle with Parmesan.

1 (3½-pound) spaghetti squash

2 tablespoons olive oil

½ teaspoon sea salt

¼ teaspoon black pepper

1 cup Alfredo Sauce (page 248)

¼ cup shredded Parmesan cheese

STORAGE

Refrigerate for up to 4 days.

TIPS & VARIATIONS

• For a nice presentation, stuff the spaghetti squash noodles back into the empty shells before serving.

• Spaghetti Squash Alfredo makes a great meatless keto meal, but if you want to add more protein, stir in some cooked shrimp or chicken before serving.

NUTRITION INFO: 371 Calories | 34.2g Fat | 10.3g Total Carbs | 1.6g Fiber | **8.7g Net Carbs** | 5.9g Protein

Unlock this recipe in the Easy Keto App →

PASTA

ZUCCHINI MANICOTTI

SERVING SIZE 3 manicotti | **SERVES 4**

Manicotti are large tubes of pasta that are stuffed with an Italian ricotta cheese mixture, topped with marinara sauce and mozzarella cheese, and baked. Zucchini manicotti is the same dish, with thinly sliced zucchini wrapped around the filling in lieu of the pasta tubes. To me, these taste even better (not to mention lighter!) than the original.

ZUCCHINI MANICOTTI NOODLES

2 pounds zucchini

3 tablespoons olive oil

½ teaspoon sea salt

¼ teaspoon black pepper

FILLING

10 ounces whole milk ricotta cheese

⅓ cup shredded mozzarella cheese

⅓ cup grated Parmesan cheese

1 large egg

1 teaspoon Italian seasoning

⅛ teaspoon sea salt

⅛ teaspoon black pepper

ASSEMBLY

1¼ cups marinara sauce, divided (½ cup and ¾ cup)

¼ cup grated Parmesan cheese

1 cup shredded mozzarella cheese

Fresh basil, for garnish, optional

STORAGE

Refrigerate for up to 5 days.

Freeze for 3 to 6 months.

Unlock this recipe in the Easy Keto App

ZUCCHINI MANICOTTI NOODLES

1. Preheat the oven to 400 degrees F. Line a baking sheet with parchment paper or foil (grease if using foil).

2. Use a mandoline to slice the zucchini into long, thin sheets, ⅛ inch thick.

3. Arrange the zucchini in a single layer on the prepared baking sheet. Brush the zucchini with olive oil, then sprinkle with salt and pepper.

4. Roast the zucchini in the oven for 15 to 20 minutes, until soft and mostly dry.

5. Remove the zucchini from the oven, but leave the oven on at 400 degrees F. Pat the zucchini with paper towels to soak up any extra moisture.

FILLING

1. In a medium bowl, stir together the filling ingredients: ricotta, mozzarella, Parmesan, egg, Italian seasoning, salt, and pepper.

ASSEMBLY

1. Spread ½ cup of the marinara sauce over the bottom of a 9 x 13-inch baking dish.

2. Arrange 3 zucchini slices at a time on a cutting board, side by side, with the long edges of the two outside pieces overlapping over the middle piece slightly. Spoon about 2 tablespoons of ricotta filling across all 3 zucchini slices toward one end, then roll up starting with that same end. Use a flat turner to carefully place into the baking dish. Repeat with the remaining zucchini slices and filling.

TIPS & VARIATIONS

· The carbs in this recipe come from vegetables, but if they are too high for your macros, try reducing the serving size to two manicotti (which would cut all the macros by one third) and pair with a protein, such as chicken or steak.

· For variations of the filling, try adding cooked chopped spinach or ground beef.

3. Spread the remaining ¾ cup of marinara sauce over the manicotti. Sprinkle each with 1 teaspoon of grated Parmesan, then 1½ tablespoons of mozzarella.

4. Bake for 15 to 20 minutes, until the cheese is melted and the filling is hot. Garnish with fresh basil ribbons, if desired.

NUTRITION INFO: 476 Calories | 33.7g Fat | 16.9g Total Carbs | 3.8g Fiber | 13.1g Net Carbs | 28.5g Protein

PASTA

VARIATIONS

- For a vegetarian version, replace the chicken broth with vegetable broth. Carb count will be a little higher, though.

- I don't use soy in my recipes, but a low-sodium soy sauce would otherwise be an okay replacement for the coconut amino,s if needed. It does actually lower the carb count a bit if you make the swap.

- This recipe makes for a light meal on its own, or you can add a protein, such as chicken, beef, pork, or shrimp, to make it a heartier meal. Sauté separately in a skillet first, remove and cover to keep warm, then proceed with the recipe as written. Add the protein and toss with sauce at the end.

VEGETABLE LO MEIN

NUT FREE

DAIRY FREE

VEGETARIAN OPTION

SERVING SIZE 1 cup | **SERVES 5**

Lo mein is a Chinese dish of noodles and vegetables tossed in sauce. Sometimes chicken, beef, pork, or shrimp is added as well. I'll be honest: My low carb version is probably more similar to Chinese-American takeout than the authentic dish, but I don't care—it's delicious! Shirataki noodles have a texture reminiscent of the type you'd expect to see in a takeout version, as long as you cook them using the method in this recipe.

1. Rinse shirataki noodles very well under cool running water.

2. Bring a pot of water to a boil. Add the noodles and boil for 3 minutes. Rinse well again under running water. Pat very dry.

3. Heat a large, heavy-bottomed skillet over medium-high heat. Add the noodles and stir-fry (without oil) for about 10 minutes, until very dry. Remove the noodles and cover to keep warm.

4. In a small bowl, whisk together the sauce: chicken broth, coconut aminos, Besti Brown, and crushed red pepper, if using. Set aside.

5. Heat olive oil in the same large skillet over medium-high heat. Add the mushrooms, bell pepper, broccoli, and garlic. Stir-fry for 5 to 8 minutes, until mushrooms are soft and peppers are tender.

6. Add the noodles and sauce to the pan. Toss to coat.

7. Increase heat to bring the sauce to a simmer. Simmer for 10 to 15 minutes, until the sauce reduces to your liking.

8. Stir in toasted sesame oil. Adjust salt and crushed red pepper to taste, if needed.

NOODLES

28 ounces (4 cups) shirataki noodles

SAUCE

½ cup chicken broth

¼ cup coconut aminos

2 tablespoons Besti Brown Monk Fruit Allulose Blend

¼ teaspoon crushed red pepper flakes, or to taste, optional

2 teaspoons toasted sesame oil

VEGETABLES

2 tablespoons olive oil

2 cups sliced mushrooms

1 large red bell pepper, sliced thinly

1½ cups broccoli florets

3 cloves garlic, minced

STORAGE

Refrigerate for up to 5 days.

NUTRITION INFO: 141 Calories | 7.6g Fat | 11.7g Total Carbs | 1.8g Fiber | 9.9g Net Carbs | 4.4g Protein

Unlock this recipe in the Easy Keto App

PASTA

NUT FREE

VEGETARIAN

3-INGREDIENT EGG NOODLES

SERVING SIZE 1 cup | **SERVES 4**

I try to avoid unfamiliar ingredients in my recipes as much as possible, but to get a noodle that has a pretty-close-to-authentic texture, it's worth it to get something a little unusual. Lupin flour is a low carb, high fiber flour made from lupin beans, which are part of the legume family (like peanuts), and can be found online. It's the key to the right texture in these noodles, so resist the urge to substitute it for something else.

½ cup lupin flour

4 large egg yolks

2 cups shredded mozzarella cheese

STORAGE

Refrigerate for up to 5 days, tossed in oil to prevent sticking.

Freeze for up to 3 months.

See Tips & Variations for instructions on storing raw noodles.

1. In a food processor, process the lupin flour and egg yolks, until uniform, dry crumbs form.

2. In a large bowl, microwave the mozzarella for about 90 seconds, or heat in a double boiler on the stove, stirring halfway through and again at the end, until smooth and easy to stir.

3. Add the cheese to the food processor, positioning the cheese so that the blades are sticking into it, and process until a dough forms. Pulse or scrape the sides as necessary.

4. Form the dough into a ball. If it's sticky, cover with plastic and refrigerate for 30 minutes, or until no longer sticky. Place the ball of dough between 2 large pieces of lightly greased parchment paper. Roll out the dough into a very thin rectangle, about ¹⁄₁₆ inch thick.

5. Peel off the top piece of parchment. Cut dough into narrow strips, about ¼ inch wide, like fettuccine. Arrange the noodles slightly apart on the parchment paper, so that they don't stick to one another.

6. Slide the parchment with the noodles onto a large baking sheet. Place in the refrigerator, uncovered, to dry out overnight, or at least 8 hours, until noodles are stiff.

7. To cook pasta, bring a pot of water to a boil. Quickly drop in the pasta and cook for about 1 minute, until pasta floats in swirls. Be careful not to overcook, or they will disintegrate.

Unlock this recipe in the Easy Keto App

NUTRITION INFO: 236 Calories | 14.5g Fat | 8.2g Total Carbs | 5.5g Fiber | **2.7g Net Carbs** | 22.7g Protein

TIPS & VARIATIONS

- Noodles will become stiff as they cool, so enjoy them while they are hot! If needed, you can reheat in the microwave, or soften them again in hot water.

- Serve noodles plain with butter or olive oil or gently toss with your favorite sauce. Try Alfredo Sauce on page 248!

- If you'll be storing raw noodles for longer than 12 hours, keep them covered on a sheet pan, so that they don't break or become more dry than needed. To store cooked noodles, toss them in oil to prevent sticking.

CHICKEN TETRAZZINI

SERVING SIZE 1 cup | **SERVES 5**

Tetrazzini is an Italian-American pasta dish featuring diced chicken (or sometimes seafood), mushrooms, and a buttery, creamy Parmesan cheese sauce. Aside from the pasta adding carbs, sauces like this are often thickened with a flour-based roux. This version swaps in my 3-Ingredient Egg Noodles (page 114), and thickens the sauce by reduction and the addition of Parmesan.

1. Season the chicken breast on both sides with salt and pepper.

2. Heat the olive oil in a 12-inch skillet over medium-high heat. Add the chicken. Sauté for 3 to 5 minutes per side, until cooked through. Remove from the pan and cover to keep warm.

3. Wipe down the pan. Add the butter and melt over medium heat. Add the mushrooms and onions and sauté for about 10 minutes, until they are soft and browned.

4. Add the garlic. Sauté for about 1 minute, until fragrant.

5. Add the chicken broth. Use a wooden spoon to scrape the browned bits from the bottom of the pan. Increase heat to bring the liquid to a boil, then reduce heat and simmer for 3 to 5 minutes, until the liquid volume is reduced by half.

6. Reduce heat to low. Add the heavy cream and Parmesan and stir, until the cheese melts and the sauce is smooth.

7. Slice the chicken into strips and return to the pan. Add the egg noodles. Use tongs to gently coat everything in sauce.

- 8 ounces boneless skinless chicken breast
- ¼ teaspoon sea salt
- ⅛ teaspoon black pepper
- 1 tablespoon olive oil
- 2 tablespoons butter
- 8 ounces button mushrooms, sliced
- ¼ large onion, diced
- 2 cloves garlic, minced
- ½ cup chicken broth
- 1 cup heavy cream
- ½ cup grated Parmesan cheese
- 1 recipe (4 cups) 3-Ingredient Egg Noodles (page 114)

STORAGE

Refrigerate for up to 4 days.

TIPS & VARIATIONS

- Though low in carbs, this meal is on the heavier side. If you want to lighten it up, feel free to use precooked zucchini noodles or spaghetti squash in place of the egg noodles.

- For a variation, try the same dish with shrimp instead of chicken; season with salt and pepper and cook for 2 to 3 minutes per side in step 2, then proceed with the recipe as written.

NUTRITION INFO: 517 Calories | 40.1g Fat | 10.9g Total Carbs | 5g Fiber | **5.9g Net Carbs** | 32.6g Protein

Unlock this recipe in the Easy Keto App

PASTA

SPAGHETTI SQUASH & SWEDISH MEATBALLS

SERVING SIZE 1 cup spaghetti squash and 6 small meatballs with sauce | **SERVES 6**

Swedish meatballs have a lot in common with their Italian counterparts, but they are smaller, include allspice and nutmeg, and are served in a creamy sauce. This low carb version uses pork rinds as a binder and cream cheese to thicken the sauce. Although meatballs can be served many ways, the carb lover's way to serve them is over pasta, so we're pairing them with spaghetti squash in this recipe.

SPAGHETTI SQUASH

1 (4-pound) spaghetti squash

1 tablespoon olive oil

¾ teaspoon sea salt

MEATBALLS

½ ounce pork rinds, crushed in a blender (makes ¼ cup)

½ teaspoon sea salt

¼ teaspoon black pepper

¼ teaspoon allspice

¼ teaspoon ground nutmeg, optional

¼ cup heavy cream

1 large egg

3 tablespoons grated onion, optional

1 pound ground beef

2 tablespoons olive oil, for frying

SAUCE

2 tablespoons butter

1 cup beef bone broth

½ cup heavy cream

4 ounces cream cheese, cut into small chunks

STORAGE

Refrigerate for up to 4 days.

1. Make spaghetti squash noodles with olive oil and sea salt according to the instructions on page 23.

2. In a large bowl, stir together the pork rinds, salt, pepper, allspice, and nutmeg, if using.

3. Whisk in the ¼ cup heavy cream, egg, and grated onion, if using.

4. Mix in the ground beef just until incorporated. Do not overmix, or else meatballs may come out tough.

5. Form the mixture into 1-inch balls. Place onto a baking sheet.

6. Heat olive oil in a large sauté pan over medium-high heat. Working in batches to avoid crowding, fry meatballs for 3 to 4 minutes per side, until browned and cooked through. Remove the meatballs to a plate and cover to keep warm.

7. Wipe out the sauté pan with a paper towel. Add the butter and melt over medium heat.

8. Add the beef bone broth and ½ cup heavy cream. Increase heat to high to bring to a boil, then reduce heat and simmer for 10 to 12 minutes, until volume is reduced by half.

9. Reduce heat to low, so that the sauce is no longer simmering. Stir in the cream cheese, until smooth. If the sauce is too thick, thin out with more cream as needed.

10. Return the meatballs to the pan and coat in sauce.

11. Serve meatballs with sauce over spaghetti squash noodles.

Unlock this recipe in the Easy Keto App

NUTRITION INFO: 581 Calories | 47.5g Fat | 13.4g Total Carbs | 2.6g Fiber | **10.8g Net Carbs** | 27.1g Protein

TIPS & VARIATIONS

· A small cookie scoop works well for forming meatballs. If using your hands, use a gentle touch and don't pack the meatballs too tightly.

· If you want the meatballs more golden, you can place them under the broiler for a couple of minutes after baking.

· I used ground beef for simplicity and to avoid adding even more ingredients, but authentic Swedish meatballs are made with a mixture of ground beef and ground pork. Feel free to use a combination if you like.

· It's fine to substitute regular beef broth for the beef bone broth, but the sauce will be less flavorful.

3-CHEESE RAVIOLI

SERVING SIZE 4 large ravioli with sauce and cheese | **SERVES 6**

Ravioli are a bit more time consuming to make than simpler keto meals, but the end result is spectacular—well worth the effort for these soft, pillowy pockets of cheesy filling! Besides, while the assembly does take some time, the advantage here is that unlike traditional frozen ravioli that take up to 10 minutes to cook, this homemade version takes only a couple of minutes in boiling water.

RAVIOLI DOUGH

1½ cups super fine blanched almond flour

2 large eggs

½ teaspoon xanthan gum

3 cups shredded mozzarella cheese

FILLING

½ cup whole milk ricotta cheese

¼ cup shredded mozzarella cheese

3 tablespoons grated Parmesan cheese

1 large egg

½ teaspoon Italian seasoning

½ teaspoon sea salt

⅛ teaspoon black pepper

ASSEMBLY

⅔ cup marinara sauce

½ cup shredded Parmesan cheese

STORAGE

Refrigerate for up to 5 days. Freeze raw for 3 to 6 months.

Unlock this recipe in the Easy Keto App
←

RAVIOLI DOUGH

1. In a food processor, pulse the almond flour, eggs, and xanthan gum, until uniform.

2. In a medium bowl in the microwave, or a double boiler on the stove, melt the mozzarella cheese, until smooth.

3. Add the melted mozzarella to the food processor. Process until a uniform dough forms. If it's sticky, cover the dough in plastic and refrigerate for at least 20 minutes, or until no longer sticky.

FILLING

1. In a medium bowl, stir together the filling ingredients: ricotta, mozzarella, Parmesan, egg, Italian seasoning, salt, and pepper.

ASSEMBLY

1. Place the ball of dough between 2 pieces of greased or lightly oiled parchment paper. Flatten into a disc, then roll into a thin rectangle, ⅛ inch thick and about 12 x 17 inches. Cut the rectangle in half across the short direction, making sure both halves are the same size and shape.

2. Use an extra small cookie scoop (2 teaspoons volume) to scoop filling onto just one of the rectangles in rows, about 1 inch apart, leaving a ½- to 1-inch empty border along the edge of the rectangle and between each scoop. You should end up with 24 scoops spaced evenly on the rectangle, with the rows and columns lined up (4 across the short side and 6 across the long side).

NUTRITION INFO: 547 Calories | 39.7g Fat | 13.5g Total Carbs | 4.5g Fiber | 9g Net Carbs | 37.8g Protein

3. Carefully place the second rectangle of dough over the first. Use your fingers to seal the outside edges and between the mounds of filling. Use a ravioli wheel, pizza wheel, or knife to cut in a grid, separating the ravioli. You should have 24 (2½-inch square) ravioli. Make sure all the edges are sealed.

4. Bring a large pot of water to a boil. Add the ravioli in a single layer, mounded side down (work in batches if necessary). Simmer for 1 to 3 minutes, until the yellowish dough turns to a lighter ivory color and they float a little higher. Be careful not to move the ravioli around or overcook so much that the dough starts to disintegrate—both can cause the ravioli to fall apart. Remove with a slotted spoon.

5. Meanwhile, heat the marinara sauce in a small saucepan.

6. To serve, spoon the marinara sauce over the ravioli and top with more shredded Parmesan cheese.

TIPS & VARIATIONS

- For a nut-free version, swap the 1½ cups almond flour with ½ cup coconut flour and add an extra egg. However, you may end up with fewer ravioli this way.

- If you want to lower carbs further, replace the marinara sauce with Alfredo Sauce (page 248) or simply butter or olive oil.

- For variations, try adding cooked chopped spinach to the ricotta filling, or swap the entire filling with cooked Italian-seasoned ground beef instead.

NUT FREE

CAULIFLOWER CARBONARA

SERVING SIZE 1 cup | **SERVES 4**

Carbonara is a pasta dish featuring a creamy sauce made with bacon or pancetta, garlic, cream, cheese, and eggs. The raw sauce is tossed in hot pasta to cook it right before serving. This low carb version swaps the pasta for roasted cauliflower, but otherwise uses exactly the same method for the sauce—and since the sauce is the star, I'll bet you won't miss the pasta too much.

1 large head cauliflower, cut into small florets

2 tablespoons olive oil

½ teaspoon sea salt

¼ teaspoon black pepper

⅓ cup heavy cream

½ cup grated Parmesan cheese

2 large eggs

1 teaspoon lemon zest

6 slices bacon, chopped into ½-inch pieces

⅓ cup frozen green peas

2 cloves garlic, minced

STORAGE

Carbonara is best fresh, as reheating will overcook the egg in the sauce.

1. Preheat the oven to 400 degrees F.

2. In a large bowl, toss the cauliflower florets with olive oil, salt, and pepper.

3. Arrange the cauliflower in a single layer on a large baking sheet. Roast in the oven for 25 to 30 minutes, until tender and browned on the edges.

4. Meanwhile, in a medium bowl, whisk together the heavy cream, Parmesan, eggs, and lemon zest. Set aside.

5. Place the bacon pieces in a cold pan on the stovetop. Turn up the heat to medium. Fry the bacon for 10 to 12 minutes, stirring occasionally, until crispy.

6. Add the frozen peas and garlic. Fry for another 1 to 2 minutes, until peas are soft and bright green.

7. Use a slotted spoon to transfer the bacon and peas to a large bowl, without the excess bacon grease. Cover to keep warm.

8. Add the roasted cauliflower to the bacon and peas. While everything is still hot, immediately pour the egg mixture over the cauliflower and very quickly toss to coat. (The heat from the cauliflower will cook the sauce.)

Unlock this recipe in the Easy Keto App

NUTRITION INFO: 414 Calories | 33.9g Fat | 12.9g Total Carbs | 4.5g Fiber | 8.4g Net Carbs | 16.7g Protein

VARIATIONS

• Peas on their own are not keto friendly but can fit most people's macros in a recipe such as this one. If you prefer to avoid them, replace them with diced green peppers.

• Traditional carbonara is made with pancetta, but I used bacon since it's usually easier to find. Feel free to use panchetta if you like!

• If you prefer the sensation of an actual noodle in your carbonara, replace the cauliflower with 3-Ingredient Egg Noodles (page 114) or Basic Spaghetti Squash Noodles (page 23). Just make sure they are piping hot when you add the sauce.

TIPS & VARIATIONS

- For easy, perfect basil ribbons, stack the whole basil leaves, roll them into tubes, and slice thinly.

- This dish can easily be made dairy-free (use dairy-free pesto and omit the Parmesan), vegetarian (skip the bacon and use olive oil instead), or nut-free (use nut-free pesto).

BACON PESTO CABBAGE NOODLES

SERVING SIZE 1 cup | **SERVES 5**

Cabbage is not the food that most carb lovers associate with noodles, but cut it into thin strips and it totally can be! Of course, this dish does taste like sautéed cabbage—mildly sweet, caramelized, and delicious. Though the taste is different, the combination of pesto, Parmesan, and long cabbage strands totally reminds me of pasta.

1. Cut the cabbage into quarters and remove the core. Cut each quarter into ½-inch-thick slices. Separate the layers, so you end up with strips. (Don't worry if some of the layers stick together; they will separate when you cook them.)

2. Place the bacon in a single layer in a large, cold sauté pan over medium heat. Cook bacon for about 10 minutes, flipping occasionally, until crispy. (Cook in batches if the bacon doesn't fit in your pan in a single layer.) Remove with tongs and set aside to drain on paper towels, leaving the bacon grease in the pan.

3. Add the onion to the pan. Fry, uncovered, for about 10 minutes, until browned.

4. Add the cabbage to the pan, cover, and cook for 15 to 20 minutes, lifting the lid to stir occasionally, until tender. If the cabbage doesn't all fit at first, add as much as possible and then add more as it cooks down. Season with salt and pepper once it starts to wilt.

5. Meanwhile, chop the bacon into small pieces.

6. When the cabbage is tender, add the pesto sauce and bacon pieces to the pan. Toss to coat. Adjust salt and pepper to taste.

7. Serve with Parmesan and fresh basil ribbons.

1 medium head cabbage (about 2½ pounds)

8 slices bacon

1 medium onion, sliced into thin half moons

¾ teaspoon sea salt

¼ teaspoon black pepper

½ cup pesto sauce

¼ cup shredded Parmesan cheese

¼ cup fresh basil ribbons

STORAGE

Refrigerate for up to 5 days.

Freeze for up to 3 months, without basil.

Unlock this recipe in the Easy Keto App

NUTRITION INFO: 350 Calories | 28.3g Fat | 14.9g Total Carbs | 5.8g Fiber | **9.1g Net Carbs** | 12.9g Protein

PASTA

ZOODLE PASTA SALAD

SERVING SIZE 1 cup | **SERVES 6**

People often think of zucchini noodles as a cooked pasta replacement, but they are also refreshing in raw salads. This zoodle pasta salad has all the flavors of an Italian pasta salad, with the zucchini noodles being the only swap. It's a perfect match for a barbecue, a quick lunch, or even a light dinner.

PASTA SALAD

2 medium zucchini, spiralized and trimmed to noodle length

1½ cups cherry tomatoes, halved

5 ounces salami, chopped

6 ounces fresh mozzarella pearls

⅓ cup pitted kalamata olives

⅓ cup red onion, sliced into quarter moons

DRESSING

¼ cup extra-virgin olive oil

1½ tablespoons red wine vinegar

¾ teaspoon Italian seasoning

¼ teaspoon sea salt

¼ teaspoon black pepper

STORAGE

Refrigerate for up to 2 days.

1. In a large bowl, toss together the spiralized zucchini, cherry tomatoes, salami, mozzarella, olives, and red onions.

2. In a small bowl, whisk together the olive oil, red wine vinegar, Italian seasoning, salt, and pepper, until emulsified.

3. Pour the dressing over the salad and toss to coat.

VARIATIONS

• For a dairy-free version, omit the mozzarella.

• For a vegetarian version, omit the salami.

• Want to change up the zucchini noodles? Try cooled roasted spaghetti squash or cauliflower florets instead.

Unlock this recipe in the Easy Keto App

NUTRITION INFO: 294 Calories | 24.7g Fat | 5.7g Total Carbs | 1.3g Fiber | 4.4g Net Carbs | 12.9g Protein

MEXICAN

TACO SALAD

SERVING SIZE 1½ cups | **SERVES 6**

Taco salad is one of my favorite weeknight meals, and once you try it, I think it will be one of yours, too! It's very easy, it uses common ingredients you're likely to have on hand, and it's ready in just 20 minutes. Plus, this dish tends to please everyone, even family and friends who aren't keto.

1. Heat the avocado oil in a large skillet over medium-high heat. Add the ground beef and cook, breaking up the pieces with a spatula, for about 7 to 10 minutes, until the beef is browned.

2. Stir in the taco seasoning and water. Cook for 2 to 3 minutes, until extra moisture evaporates and a sauce forms.

3. Meanwhile, in a large bowl, combine the lettuce, tomatoes, Cheddar, avocado, and green onions.

4. Add the ground beef, salsa, and sour cream. Toss everything together to combine.

1 teaspoon avocado oil

1 pound ground beef

2 tablespoons taco seasoning

¼ cup water

8 ounces romaine lettuce, chopped

1⅓ cups cherry tomatoes, halved

¾ cup shredded Cheddar cheese

1 medium avocado, cubed

½ cup chopped green onions

⅓ cup salsa

⅓ cup sour cream

TIPS & VARIATIONS

• I used my homemade taco seasoning recipe for this recipe: **www.wholesomeyum.com/gluten-free-keto-low-carb-taco-seasoning-recipe**. You can use store-bought seasoning instead if you like, but watch for added sugar, and if it does not contain salt, add 1 teaspoon of sea salt.

• For a dairy-free version, omit the Cheddar and use dairy-free sour cream (or even coconut cream with a bit of salt).

• Ground beef can be substituted for any protein you enjoy on tacos, such as chicken breast or thighs, ground turkey, fish, or shrimp. Just toss in taco seasoning and sauté until cooked through.

• Customize the veggies in your salad to your liking! Bell peppers, cucumbers, red onions, and cooked summer squash all make delicious additions. Avoid corn and beans, which are high in carbs.

STORAGE

Taco salad is best fresh, but you can chop the components (except avocado) up to 2 days ahead.

NUTRITION INFO: 410 Calories | 30.7g Fat | 8.9g Total Carbs | 4.4g Fiber | 4.5g Net Carbs | 27.2g Protein

Unlock this recipe in the Easy Keto App

MEXICAN

STEAK BURRITO BOWLS

SERVING SIZE 1 bowl, or ¼ entire recipe | **SERVES 4**

A burrito bowl is very similar to a Taco Salad (see page 131), but it's served over rice (in this case, Cilantro Lime Cauliflower Rice!) instead of lettuce. This version also gets an upgrade with thinly sliced steak instead of the more common ground beef option.

1 pound flank steak, sliced thinly against the grain

2 tablespoons olive oil, divided in half

1 tablespoon lime juice

1 tablespoon taco seasoning

1 recipe (4 cups) Cilantro Lime Cauliflower Rice (page 69)

4 medium roma tomatoes, seeded and diced

¼ large red onion, diced

1 medium avocado, sliced

¼ cup sour cream

STORAGE

Refrigerate for up to 3 days, without avocado.

Freeze for up to 3 months, without fresh vegetables and sour cream.

1. In a large bowl, toss the sliced steak with 1 tablespoon olive oil, lime juice, and taco seasoning.

2. Heat the remaining tablespoon of olive oil in a large skillet over medium-high heat, until shimmering. Add the steak in a single layer and cook for 2 to 3 minutes per side, until browned on both sides.

3. Divide the cauliflower rice into 4 bowls, 1 cup each. Top with steak, tomatoes, onions, avocado, and sour cream.

TIPS & VARIATIONS

- I used my homemade taco seasoning for this recipe: **www.wholesomeyum.com/gluten-free-keto-low-carb-taco-seasoning-recipe**. You can use store-bought seasoning instead if you like, but watch for added sugar, and if it does not contain salt, add ½ teaspoon of sea salt.

- For a dairy-free version, simply omit the sour cream.

- If you have time, marinate the steak in the oil, lime juice, and seasoning for at least 1 to 2 hours (but no longer than 24 hours) before cooking. This will make the dish even more flavorful.

- Burrito bowls also work with other proteins, such as chicken breast or thighs, ground turkey, fish, or shrimp. If you use seafood, however, be sure not to marinate for longer than 30 minutes.

Unlock this recipe in the Easy Keto App

NUTRITION INFO: 472 Calories | 34.1g Fat | 16.2g Total Carbs | 7.4g Fiber | 8.8g Net Carbs | 28.8g Protein

ZUCCHINI TORTILLAS

SERVING SIZE 1 tortilla | **SERVES 4**

NUT FREE

VEGETARIAN

Zucchini tortillas sneak shredded zucchini into a neutral-flavored, pliable wrap that you can bend and use almost like a regular tortilla. Not only are these low in carbs, they are also pretty light on calories and a surprisingly great source of protein. Coconut flour's absorbent properties are crucial here to balance the moisture from the zucchini, so substitutions are not recommended.

1. Preheat the oven to 400 degrees F. Line two baking sheets with parchment paper.

2. Place the zucchini in a colander and toss with salt. Sit the colander in the sink and let the zucchini drain for 30 minutes.

3. After 30 minutes, wrap the zucchini in a tea towel and squeeze to release as much moisture as possible. (Between the draining and squeezing, the zucchinishould release at least ¼ cup of water.)

4. In a large bowl, whisk the eggs. Stir in the coconut flour and Italian seasoning.

5. Sprinkle (don't dump) xanthan gum evenly over the bowl, then stir in.

6. Add the zucchini and mozzarella. Stir until uniform.

7. Divide the mixture into 4 portions and drop onto the prepared baking sheets, 2 scoops per sheet, at least 6 inches apart. Use a spatula or the back of a spoon to spread into thin, smooth circles, about 7 inches in diameter. Bake for about 15 minutes, rotating the pans halfway through, until the edges are dry and tortillas are golden. Cool for 10 minutes before moving.

1 pound zucchini, shredded

¼ teaspoon sea salt

3 large eggs

2 tablespoons coconut flour

1 teaspoon Italian seasoning

¼ teaspoon xanthan gum

¾ cup shredded mozzarella cheese

STORAGE

Refrigerate for up to 5 days.

Freeze for 3 to 6 months, with parchment paper between tortillas.

VARIATIONS

• Mozzarella produces the most neutral-tasting results, but other cheeses that melt well, such as Cheddar or Pepper Jack, would also work if you don't mind the stronger flavor.

• If you plan to use the tortillas for a Mexican dish, try swapping the Italian seasoning for garlic powder, ground cumin, paprika, and/or chili powder.

NUTRITION INFO: 144 Calories | 7.8g Fat | 6.9g Total Carbs | 3g Fiber | 3.9g Net Carbs | 11.9g Protein

Unlock this recipe in the Easy Keto App

MEXICAN

NUT FREE

TURKEY ENCHILADA ZUCCHINI BOATS

SERVING SIZE 2 zucchini boats | **SERVES 4**

For enchilada zucchini boats, we stuff saucy ground turkey enchilada filling into partially hollowed-out roasted zucchini instead of the traditional flour tortilla. They are healthy, sweet, spicy, and actually much easier to make than regular enchiladas, anyway.

4 medium zucchini

2 tablespoons olive oil, divided in half

⅓ cup diced onion

1 pound ground turkey

1 teaspoon sea salt, divided (¼ teaspoon and ¾ teaspoon)

¼ teaspoon black pepper

1 (10-ounce) can diced tomatoes with green chilies, drained

1 cup enchilada sauce

1 cup Mexican cheese blend

STORAGE

Refrigerate for up to 5 days.

Freeze for 3 to 6 months.

1. Preheat the oven to 400 degrees F. Line a baking sheet with foil or parchment paper.

2. Slice the zucchini lengthwise. Use a spoon or melon baller to scoop out the seedy parts of the centers of the zucchini to make wells.

3. Place the zucchini on the baking sheet, cut side up. Drizzle with 1 tablespoon of the olive oil and sprinkle ¼ teaspoon salt lightly over all the zucchini.

4. Roast the zucchini in the oven for about 15 to 20 minutes, until fork tender.

5. Meanwhile, heat another tablespoon of olive oil in a large nonstick skillet over medium-high heat. Add the diced onions. Sauté for about 7 to 10 minutes, until starting to brown.

6. Add the ground turkey. Season with pepper and the remaining ¾ teaspoon salt. Cook for about 10 minutes, breaking apart with a spatula, until browned.

7. Stir in the diced tomatoes with green chilies and enchilada sauce. Increase heat to bring to a gentle boil, then simmer for 5 to 7 minutes, until excess sauce absorbs into the meat.

8. When the zucchini are done, remove from the oven and leave the oven on at 400 degrees F.

9. Use paper towels to pat any moisture from the zucchini boats. Spoon the turkey mixture inside, then sprinkle with cheese.

10. Bake for about 5 minutes, until the cheese is melted.

Unlock this recipe in the Easy Keto App

←

NUTRITION INFO: 405 Calories | 26.1g Fat | 13.9g Total Carbs | 4.2g Fiber | 9.7g Net Carbs | 31.4g Protein

TIPS & VARIATIONS

• I use homemade enchilada
sauce for this recipe:
**www.wholesomeyum.com/
recipes/easy-gluten-free-
enchilada-sauce-recipe**.
If you decide to make it,
start the enchilada sauce
first and let it simmer while
you prepare the zucchini.
A store-bought version
without added sugar works
fine as well.

• If you would like a milder,
less spicy filling, stir in
2 ounces of cream cheese
after cooking the meat
sauce, before filling the
zucchini.

TIPS & VARIATIONS

- I used my homemade taco seasoning for this recipe: **www.wholesomeyum.com/ gluten-free-keto-low-carb-taco-seasoning-recipe**. You can use store-bought seasoning instead if you like, but watch for added sugar, and if it does not contain salt, add ½ teaspoon of sea salt.

- The serving size listed makes a good snack or appetizer. Double or triple it for a full meal instead.

- Feel free to swap the ground beef with your favorite protein, like chicken breast or thighs, ground turkey, fish, or shrimp. Just toss in taco seasoning and sauté until cooked through.

CHEESE TACO CUPS

NUT FREE

SERVING SIZE 1 taco cup | **SERVES 12**

You can't go wrong with these versatile cheese taco cups! The shells are made from crispy Cheddar cheese, and you can customize the cups with any of your favorite taco fillings. The cup format makes for a beautiful presentation for party appetizers, or enjoy a few for an easy Mexican meal.

CHEESE CUPS

1. Preheat the oven to 400 degrees F. Line an extra-large baking sheet with parchment paper.

2. Scoop 12 mounds of Cheddar onto the parchment paper, about 2 tablespoons each and 3 inches in diameter, 2 inches apart.

3. Bake for 5 to 7 minutes, until the edges are golden brown. (Watch carefully, they go from golden edges to burned quickly.) Let the cheese cool for 1 to 2 minutes, until it's no longer gooey but still pliable.

4. Working quickly before the cheese cools too much, gently lift the cheese rounds and press into a muffin tin, forming 12 cups. Set aside to cool.

FILLING

1. Heat avocado oil in a medium skillet over medium-high heat. Add ground beef and cook, breaking up the pieces with a spatula, for about 6 to 8 minutes, until the beef is browned.

2. Stir in taco seasoning and water. Cook for 1 to 2 minutes, until extra moisture evaporates and a sauce forms.

ASSEMBLY

1. Divide the taco meat among the cheese cups.

2. Top each cup with sour cream, diced tomatoes, followed by diced onions, avocado, and chopped cilantro.

CHEESE CUPS

1½ cups shredded Cheddar cheese

FILLING

1 teaspoon avocado oil

½ pound ground beef

1 tablespoon taco seasoning

2 tablespoons water

TOPPINGS

¼ cup sour cream

¼ cup plus 2 tablespoons diced fresh tomatoes

3 tablespoons diced red onion

½ large avocado, diced

1 tablespoon chopped cilantro

STORAGE

Taco cups are best fresh; the cheese shells will melt if you reheat them.

Unlock this recipe in the Easy Keto App

MEXICAN

NUTRITION INFO: 145 Calories | 11.3g Fat | 2g Total Carbs | 0.9g Fiber | 1.1g Net Carbs | 9.3g Protein

CHICKEN TAQUITOS

SERVING SIZE 2 taquitos | **SERVES 4**

Taquitos are rolled up tacos that are filled with beef or chicken and crisp-fried or deep-fried. They were one of my go-to freezer meals in college, but making your own is a lot healthier—and tastier. This low carb version has just a handful of ingredients in the filling and uses cheese to form crispy wraps. No deep-frying required!

FILLING

1 tablespoon avocado oil

2 cloves garlic, minced

1½ cups cooked chicken, shredded

1 (14½-ounce) can diced tomatoes, with liquid

1 tablespoon taco seasoning

1½ ounces cream cheese, cubed

CHEESE WRAPS

1½ cups shredded Cheddar cheese

1½ cups shredded Colby Jack cheese

½ teaspoon ground cumin

STORAGE

Refrigerate for up to 5 days.

Freeze for 3 to 6 months.

Watch closely when reheating, or the cheese shells will melt.

FILLING

1. Heat the avocado oil in a medium skillet over medium heat. Add the garlic and sauté for about 30 seconds, until fragrant.

2. Add the chicken, diced tomatoes (with liquid), and taco seasoning. Increase heat to bring to a boil, then reduce heat and simmer for 3 to 5 minutes, until the extra liquid is absorbed into the chicken.

3. Reduce heat to low. Stir in the cream cheese, pressing with the back of a spoon or spatula to help it mix in, until melted and smooth. Cover to keep warm.

CHEESE WRAPS & ASSEMBLY

1. Meanwhile, preheat the oven to 400 degrees F. Line 2 large baking sheets with parchment paper.

2. In a large bowl, mix the Cheddar and Colby Jack together. Divide the cheese into 8 round circles on the prepared baking sheets, about ⅓ cup cheese per circle, 4 inches in diameter, at least 2 inches apart. Sprinkle lightly with cumin.

3. Bake for 6 to 8 minutes, until the cheese is golden around the edges but still pale and bubbly in the center. Let the cheese circles cool on the baking sheet for 2 to 3 minutes, until no longer gooey but still pliable.

4. Working quickly before the cheese hardens too much, place 2 to 3 tablespoons of filling in a line down the center of each cheese circle and roll up.

Unlock this recipe in the Easy Keto App

NUTRITION INFO: 554 Calories | 40.8g Fat | 9.2g Total Carbs | 1.6g Fiber | 7.6g Net Carbs | 36.4g Protein

TIPS & VARIATIONS

- I used my homemade taco seasoning for this recipe: **www.wholesomeyum.com/gluten-free-keto-low-carb-taco-seasoning-recipe**. You can use store-bought seasoning instead if you like, but watch for added sugar, and if it does not contain salt, add ½ teaspoon of sea salt.

- Serve taquitos with shredded lettuce, guacamole, salsa, sour cream, and cilantro.

- Make beef taquitos by swapping the shredded chicken for cooked ground beef.

- For a healthy crunch in the filling, add diced bell peppers or onions.

TIPS & VARIATIONS

• I use my homemade taco seasoning for this recipe: **www.wholesomeyum.com/ gluten-free-keto-low-carb-taco-seasoning-recipe**. You can use store-bought seasoning instead if you like, but watch for added sugar, and if it does not contain salt, add 1 teaspoon of sea salt.

• If you want to simplify this recipe or don't like cilantro, feel free to replace the Cilantro Lime Cauliflower Rice with plain cooked cauliflower rice (seasoned with salt and pepper).

• One stuffed pepper makes a generous, filling meal. If you want to lighten it up, cut the peppers lengthwise instead of removing the tops. Filling the halves separately will yield a smaller portion size and double the number of servings.

• Halving the portion size as suggested above will give you room in your macros for toppings, if you like them! Try sour cream, avocado, sliced jalapeños, and fresh cilantro.

MEXICAN BEEF & RICE STUFFED PEPPERS

SERVING SIZE 1 stuffed pepper | **SERVES 6**

Stuffed peppers make a naturally low carb meal when you fill them with meat and cheese, but this version for carb lovers also adds cauliflower rice to the filling. It makes an even more satisfying meal that way!

1. Preheat the oven to 400 degrees F.

2. To prepare the peppers, chop off the tops and scoop out the seeds and ribs inside. Slice a tiny layer off the bottoms (without making a hole, if possible) so that the peppers are stable standing upright.

3. Place the peppers in a baking dish, open side up. Drizzle with 2 tablespoons of the olive oil and sprinkle with salt.

4. Bake peppers for about 15 minutes, until they are soft and the edges are slightly puckered. Remove from the oven and reduce heat to 350 degrees F. Using paper towels, blot any extra liquid inside the peppers.

5. Meanwhile, prepare the filling. In a large sauté pan, heat the remaining tablespoon of olive oil over medium heat. Add the diced red onions and sauté for 5 to 10 minutes, until translucent and slightly golden.

6. Push the onions to the sides of the pan and add the ground beef in the center. Cook, breaking apart with a spatula, for 8 to 10 minutes, until cooked through.

7. Add the taco seasoning and water to the pan. Simmer for 3 to 4 minutes, until the extra liquid evaporates.

8. Stir in the diced tomatoes and cauliflower rice.

9. Spoon the filling into the pepper, halfway full. Sprinkle with about 2 to 3 tablespoons of the shredded cheese. Top with the remaining filling and cheese.

10. Return to the oven for 7 to 10 minutes, until the cheese is melted.

6 large bell peppers

3 tablespoons olive oil, divided (2 tablespoons and 1 tablespoon)

¼ teaspoon sea salt

⅓ cup diced red onions

1 pound ground beef

2 tablespoons taco seasoning

½ cup water

1 (14½-ounce) can diced tomatoes, drained

2 cups Cilantro Lime Cauliflower Rice (page 69)

2 cups shredded Cheddar cheese

STORAGE

Refrigerate for up to 5 days.

Freeze for 3 to 6 months.

NUTRITION INFO: 576 Calories | 41.2g Fat | 18.5g Total Carbs | 5.8g Fiber | 12.7g Net Carbs | 33.6g Protein

Unlock this recipe in the Easy Keto App

MEXICAN

TEX-MEX MIGAS

SERVING SIZE 1 cup | **SERVES 6**

Migas are a Tex-Mex egg dish made by frying up strips of corn tortillas before mixing them with scrambled eggs, peppers, onions, and cheese. Salsa is also often involved, along with plenty of fun toppings. This low carb version uses Rutabaga Chips (page 180) in lieu of the tortilla strips and keeps the ingredient list to a minimum, while capturing the same essence.

10 large eggs

⅓ cup heavy cream

½ teaspoon sea salt

⅛ teaspoon black pepper

1 tablespoon olive oil

½ small onion, diced

1 large bell pepper, seeded and diced

1 medium jalapeño pepper, seeded and minced

1 recipe (3 cups) Rutabaga Chips (page 180), cut into strips or crumbled

¾ cup shredded Cheddar cheese, divided (½ cup and ¼ cup)

STORAGE

Migas are best fresh; chips will get soggy if not eaten right away.

1. In a large bowl, whisk together the eggs, heavy cream, salt, and pepper. Set aside.

2. Heat olive oil in a large sauté pan over medium heat. Add the diced onion, bell pepper, and jalapeño. Sauté for 10 to 12 minutes, until vegetables are soft and starting to brown.

3. Add the egg mixture and cook, stirring frequently, for about 3 minutes, until scrambled.

4. Reduce heat to low. Stir in the chips and ½ cup of the Cheddar. Sprinkle the remaining ¼ cup of Cheddar on top. Cover and cook for about 2 minutes, until the cheese melts.

TIPS & VARIATIONS

• Load up your migas with your favorite low carb toppings! Mine are avocado, chopped cilantro, and a squeeze of lime. Beans wouldn't be keto friendly, but you can try diced tomatoes, diced red onions, sliced radishes, salsa, hot sauce, or crumbled Cotija cheese.

• If you enjoy spicy food, double the amount of jalapeños.

• Chips are an integral part of migas, but if these don't work with your macros, you can omit them to make this recipe into spicy, cheesy scrambled eggs with veggies instead.

Unlock this recipe in the Easy Keto App

NUTRITION INFO: 379 Calories | 29.6g Fat | 14.1g Total Carbs | 3.7g Fiber | **10.4g Net Carbs** | 15.6g Protein

FRIED FOODS

TIPS & VARIATIONS

- Be sure your whey protein powder has zero carbs and sugar, otherwise they can add up fast in this recipe.

- Although I often suggest egg white protein powder as a substitute for whey protein powder, it's not recommended for these onion rings (or any other recipe where whey is used in breading), because the result will be chewy instead of crispy.

- When dipping and dredging the onion rings, use one hand for the dry ingredients and the other for the wet. This will help reduce clumping.

- For a classic dipping sauce, whisk together ½ cup mayonnaise, 1 tablespoon ketchup, 1 tablespoon creamy horseradish, 1 teaspoon paprika, and salt and pepper to taste.

DEEP-FRIED ONION RINGS

SERVING SIZE about 4 to 5 onion rings, or ⅙ entire recipe | **SERVES 6**

Coated with a white flour batter and commonly cooked in canola oil, deep-fried onion rings are one of the unhealthiest appetizers on restaurant menus. This recipe gives them a healthier makeover, without giving up the crispy exterior you love.

1. Heat avocado oil in a Dutch oven to 350 degrees F. (Be careful not to overheat—sometimes cast iron continues to rise in temperature.)

2. In a large bowl, stir together the whey protein powder, almond flour, baking powder, salt, and pepper. Add the eggs and sparkling water. Whisk to combine into a batter.

3. Place the coconut flour in a small bowl. Dredge the onion rings individually in the coconut flour, then dip into the batter to coat. Let the excess batter drip off and add the onion to the hot oil. Working in batches, repeat with the remaining onion rings, keeping them in a single layer in the pan (don't crowd the pan). Fry for 1 to 2 minutes per side, until golden brown. Remove with a slotted spoon and drain on paper towels.

3 to 4 cups avocado oil

1⅓ cups whey protein powder

⅔ cup super fine blanched almond flour

2 teaspoons baking powder

1 teaspoon sea salt

½ teaspoon black pepper

2 large eggs, whisked

½ cup sparkling water, cold

3 tablespoons coconut flour

1 large white onion, sliced and separated into ½-inch rings

STORAGE

Onion rings are best fresh; the breading will get soft if they are not eaten right away.

NUTRITION INFO: 416 Calories | 35.9g Fat | 7.7g Total Carbs | 3.3g Fiber | 4.4g Net Carbs | 17.9g Protein

Nutrition info only includes the ¾ cup of oil that gets absorbed into the onion rings; the rest is discarded.

Unlock this recipe in the Easy Keto App

FRIED FOODS

BAKED FRIED CHICKEN

SERVING SIZE 1 drumstick | **SERVES 6**

These "fried" chicken drumsticks are a family favorite! They are perfectly crispy on the outside, juicy on the inside, and very simple to prepare. Baking makes this recipe easier and lighter, but see the Variations on the opposite page if you prefer frying.

¼ cup coconut flour

½ teaspoon sea salt

¼ teaspoon black pepper

2 large eggs

2 ounces pork rinds, crushed in a blender (makes 1 cup)

2 tablespoons whey protein powder

½ tablespoon smoked paprika

1 teaspoon poultry seasoning

½ teaspoon garlic powder

6 chicken drumsticks (about 2½ pounds)

STORAGE

Refrigerate for up to 5 days.
Freeze for 3 to 6 months.

1. Preheat the oven to 400 degrees F. Place an oven-safe wire rack over a baking sheet.

2. Prep your dredging station with 3 medium bowls: In the first bowl, stir together the coconut flour, salt, and pepper. In the second bowl, whisk together the eggs. In a third bowl, mix the crushed pork rinds, whey protein powder, smoked paprika, poultry seasoning, and garlic powder.

3. Dredge the drumsticks in the coconut flour mixture, dip in the eggs, gently shake off the excess, then press into the pork rind mixture. To prevent clumping, keep most of the pork rind mixture in a separate bowl and add a little at a time to a fourth bowl where you'll be coating the chicken.

4. Arrange the drumsticks in a single layer on the rack fitted over the baking sheet. Bake for 25 to 35 minutes, until golden on the outside and internal temperature reaches 165 degrees F. Drain on paper towels.

Unlock this recipe in the Easy Keto App

←

NUTRITION INFO: 223 Calories | 12.4g Fat | 3.4g Total Carbs | 2.2g Fiber | 1.2g Net Carbs | 23g Protein

VARIATIONS

- For a dairy-free version, sub the whey protein powder with more pork rinds. However, the texture is better with the protein powder included.

- When dipping and dredging the chicken, use one hand for the dry ingredients and the other for the wet. This will help reduce clumping.

- You can use store-bought poultry seasoning, or use my homemade version for this recipe: **www.wholesomeyum.com/ poultry-seasoning**.

- Feel free to use other cuts of chicken if that's what you have on hand. The breading is enough for 6 pieces, on average.

- Baking is the easiest way to make this chicken, but you can also fry it in heat-safe oil, such as avocado oil, if you prefer. Heat the oil (enough to deep-fry the chicken) to 350 degrees F first, then add the chicken and fry for 7 to 12 minutes per side, until internal temperature reaches 165 degrees F.

CRISPY MOZZARELLA STICKS

SERVING SIZE **4 mozzarella sticks** | SERVES 6

With a cheesy, gooey interior with a crispy coating, this keto friendly take on mozzarella sticks is sure to fulfill every carb-y comfort food craving! Making these is also a fun activity to do with kids—they can help with the stirring and dipping.

1. Line a baking sheet with parchment paper. Set aside.

2. Prep your dredging station with 3 small bowls: In the first bowl, place coconut flour. In the second bowl, whisk the egg. In the third bowl, mix the almond flour, crushed pork rinds, Italian seasoning, and garlic powder, if using.

3. Dredge a piece of mozzarella in coconut flour, dip in the egg, then gently shake off the excess. Roll in the almond flour mixture until well coated, then place on the prepared baking sheet. Repeat with all the mozzarella (don't let the pieces touch on the baking sheet).

4. Place the baking sheet in the freezer for at least one hour, or until ready to fry. (This is critical to prevent the cheese from oozing out during frying.)

5. Heat avocado oil in a skillet over medium heat. Working in batches, fry the mozzarella sticks in a single layer, 1 to 2 minutes per side. They are done when they are golden brown and soft inside when pressed gently.

2 tablespoons coconut flour

1 large egg

½ cup super fine blanched almond flour

1 ounce pork rinds, crushed in a blender (makes ½ cup)

2 teaspoons Italian seasoning

½ teaspoon garlic powder, optional

12 pieces mozzarella string cheese, halved crosswise

2 tablespoons avocado oil

STORAGE

Fried mozzarella sticks are best eaten fresh.

Freeze uncooked for 3 to 6 months.

TIPS

• When dipping and dredging the mozzarella sticks, use one hand for the dry ingredients and the other for the wet. This will help reduce clumping.

• You can batch prep this recipe and store the uncooked, breaded mozzarella sticks in the freezer until you're ready to fry them. Freeze on a parchment-lined baking sheet first, then transfer to a freezer bag once they are solid.

NUTRITION INFO: 250 Calories | 18.6g Fat | 5.9g Total Carbs | 2.1g Fiber | 3.8g Net Carbs | 16.8g Protein

Unlock this recipe in the Easy Keto App

CINNAMON CHURROS

SERVING SIZE 1 (3-inch) churro | **SERVES 20**

When my husband and I visited Spain, churros were my favorite dessert to splurge on—and for good reason: so that I could create a keto version when I returned home. This churro recipe follows a similar process to the original, swapping in keto friendly ingredients. The churros turn out crispy on the outside, chewy on the inside, and have the best sweet cinnamon coating.

DOUGH

½ cup water

6 tablespoons butter

2 tablespoon Besti Monk Fruit Allulose Blend

½ teaspoon sea salt

½ teaspoon xanthan gum

1¾ cups super fine blanched almond flour

½ cup whey protein powder

1 large egg, at room temperature

1 teaspoon vanilla extract

1½ cups avocado oil

COATING

¼ cup Besti Monk Fruit Allulose Blend

½ teaspoon ground cinnamon

STORAGE

Refrigerate for up to 5 days.

Freeze for 3 to 6 months.

1. In a large saucepan over medium-high heat, combine the water, butter, Besti, and salt. Bring to a boil.

2. Turn off heat. Sprinkle (don't dump) in the xanthan gum. Add the almond flour and whey protein powder. Stir continuously with a rubber spatula, until a ball of dough forms.

3. Transfer the mixture to a large bowl. Cool for 10 minutes.

4. Using a hand mixer, beat in the egg and vanilla extract.

5. Transfer the mixture into a piping bag fitted with an extra-large star tip.

6. Heat avocado oil in a large saucepan over medium heat, or medium-low if using cast iron. (The oil should be about 1½ inches deep and register about 325 to 350 degrees F.)

7. Working in batches to avoid crowding the pan, pipe the mixture into the preheated oil, using scissors to cut the churro strips to about 3 inches long. Do not let the pieces touch. Fry until golden, about 1 to 2 minutes per side. Transfer to a paper-towel-lined plate to drain. Let the churros cool for about 2 minutes, until not too hot to handle.

8. In a medium shallow bowl, stir together Besti and cinnamon for the coating. Roll churros in the mixture.

Unlock this recipe in the Easy Keto App ←

NUTRITION INFO: 144 Calories | 14g Fat | 2.2g Total Carbs | 1.1g Fiber | 1.1g Net Carbs | 3.8g Protein

Nutrition info includes only the ½ cup of oil that gets absorbed into the churros; the rest is discarded.

TIPS & VARIATIONS

• For a dairy-free version, substitute egg white protein powder for the whey protein powder and unrefined coconut oil for the butter.

• Extra-large piping tips work best for a classic churro size. If you use a regular-size tip, your churros will cook much faster and sometimes burn more easily.

• Churros are delicious plain but even better dipped in sugar-free chocolate sauce! Find the recipe at: **www.wholesomeyum.com/ sugar-free-chocolate-syrup**.

TIPS & VARIATIONS

- For a dairy-free version, substitute more pork rinds for the whey protein powder. However, the texture is better with the protein powder included. In the sauce, you can substitute ghee or coconut oil for butter.

- When dipping and dredging the chicken, use one hand for the dry ingredients and the other for the wet. This will help reduce clumping.

- For a classic presentation, serve buffalo wings with blue cheese or ranch dressing and celery sticks.

- The same breaded chicken base works great with other sauces! Try swapping the buffalo-butter sauce with sugar-free BBQ sauce; find the recipe at: **www.whole someyum.com/recipes/ low-carb-bbq-sauce- sugar-free-gluten-free**.

BONELESS BUFFALO WINGS

SERVING SIZE 4 pieces | **SERVES 6**

One of my favorite casual restaurants used to be a place known for its boneless buffalo wings. Needless to say, those were far from keto friendly, but experimenting with low carb breading options has led me to create a homemade version that's just as crispy and spicy. It will remind you of your favorite wing joint!

1. Prep your dredging station with 3 medium bowls: In the first bowl, stir together the coconut flour, salt, and pepper. In the second bowl, whisk together the eggs. In a third bowl, mix the crushed pork rinds, whey protein powder, paprika, and garlic powder.

2. Dredge the chicken pieces in the coconut flour mixture, dip in the eggs, gently shake off the excess, then press into the pork rind mixture. To prevent clumping, keep most of the third mixture in a separate bowl and add a little at a time to a fourth bowl where you'll be coating the chicken.

3. Refrigerate the breaded chicken for 20 minutes.

4. Heat 1½ inches of avocado oil in a 3½-quart saucepan over medium-high heat, until it reaches 350 degrees F. Working in batches, fry the chicken in a single layer, 2 to 3 minutes per side, until golden on the outside and internal temperature reaches 165 degrees F. Drain on paper towels.

5. In a small bowl, combine the buffalo sauce and butter. Heat in the microwave or gently on the stove, until the butter melts. Stir until smooth.

6. Transfer the breaded chicken to a large bowl. Pour the buffalo sauce mixture evenly over the chicken and use tongs to coat gently.

BONELESS WINGS

¼ cup coconut flour

½ teaspoon sea salt

¼ teaspoon black pepper

2 large eggs

2 ounces pork rinds, crushed in a blender (makes 1 cup)

2 tablespoons whey protein powder

1 teaspoon paprika

½ teaspoon garlic powder

1 pound boneless skinless chicken breasts, cut into 1½- to 2-inch pieces

3 cups avocado oil

SAUCE

⅔ cup buffalo sauce

⅓ cup butter

STORAGE

Refrigerate for up to 5 days.

Freeze for 3 to 6 months.

For best results, do not mix wings with sauce before storing.

NUTRITION INFO: 356 Calories | 29.6g Fat | 3.1g Total Carbs | 2.2g Fiber | 0.9g Net Carbs | 26.7g Protein

Nutrition info includes only the ⅓ cup oil that gets absorbed into the chicken; the rest is discarded.

Unlock this recipe in the Easy Keto App

FRIED FOODS

FISH & CHIPS

SERVING SIZE 5 ounces fish (1 fillet) and 10 fries, or ¼ entire recipe | **SERVES 4**

Like many of my recipes, this one was inspired by my travels. Fish and chips were everywhere when my husband and I visited England, where I learned a thing or two about how this dish is prepared. My low carb version might not be 100% authentic, but the batter results in a super-crispy breading, just like the real thing.

½ recipe (4 servings) Rutabaga Fries (page 66)

3 to 4 cups avocado oil

3 tablespoons coconut flour

⅔ cup whey protein powder

⅓ cup super fine blanched almond flour

1 teaspoon baking powder

½ teaspoon sea salt

¼ teaspoon black pepper

1 large egg, whisked

¼ cup sparkling water, cold

4 (5-ounce) cod fillets

STORAGE

Fried fish is best fresh; the breading will get soft if the fish is not eaten right away.

1. Make the rutabaga fries according to the instructions on page 66. While the fries are baking, make the fish.

2. Heat oil in a Dutch oven to 350 degrees F. (Be careful not to overheat—sometimes cast iron continues to rise in temperature.)

3. In a large bowl, stir together the whey protein powder, almond flour, baking powder, salt, and pepper. Add the eggs and sparkling water. Whisk to combine into a batter. Place the coconut flour in a small bowl.

4. Dredge the cod fillets in the coconut flour, then dip into the batter to coat. Let the excess batter drip off and add the fish to the hot oil. Repeat with the remaining fillets, making sure not to crowd the pan. Fry fish for 2 minutes per side, until golden brown.

5. Serve fish with rutabaga fries.

Unlock this recipe in the Easy Keto App

NUTRITION INFO: 588 Calories | 42g Fat | 13.9g Total Carbs | 5.5g Fiber | 8.4g Net Carbs | 39.9g Protein

Nutrition info includes both the fish and fries. Only ½ cup of oil that gets absorbed into the fish is included; the rest is discarded.

TIPS & VARIATIONS

- You can use any kind of flaky white fish, such as cod, walleye, and catfish. Frozen fish is fine, but thaw it first.

- Although I often suggest egg white protein powder as a substitute for whey protein powder, it's not recommended for fried fish (or any other recipe where whey is used in breading), because the result will be chewy instead of crispy.

- Since it's deep-fried, this is a heavier meal. Feel free to lightly panfry instead, or serve with a light salad instead of the fries.

- If you want to serve Fish & Chips with tartar sauce, it's best to make your own, as the ones in the store contain sugar. Find the recipe at: **www.wholesomeyum.com/keto-tartar-sauce**.

TIPS & VARIATIONS

- For a vegetarian version, you can replace the pork rinds with blanched almond flour. However, the falafel will be less crispy this way.

- Serve falafel with plain Cauliflower Rice (page 17) or a salad of tomatoes, cucumbers, feta, olive oil, and fresh herbs. Tahini sauce is also a popular pairing. Get the recipe here: **www.wholesomeyum.com/ tahini-sauce-recipe**.

CAULIFLOWER FALAFEL

SERVING SIZE 6 pieces | **SERVES 6**

Falafel is a Middle Eastern street food traditionally made by forming patties out of chickpeas, herbs, and spices and frying them. The best I've ever had was in Israel. Like other beans, chickpeas are not keto friendly, but—surprise—you can actually mimic a similar flavor and texture by combining cauliflower with the same herbs and spices!

1. In a food processor, intermittently pulse cauliflower, garlic, onion, parsley, cilantro, lemon zest, ½ cup of the crushed pork rinds, cumin, salt, cayenne pepper, and eggs, until a coarsely textured meal forms. (Be careful not to overmix—you don't want the mixture to be smooth.)

2. Line a baking sheet with parchment paper. Scoop 1 tablespoon of the mixture and, using wet hands, form a disc about 1½ inches in diameter and ½ inch thick. Roll in remaining ¼ cup of pork rinds. Place onto the prepared baking sheet and repeat with the rest of the mixture. You should end up with 36 discs in a single layer on the baking sheet.

3. Refrigerate for 1 hour.

4. Heat ½ inch of olive oil in a large skillet over medium-low to medium heat, until shimmering. Working in batches, add the falafel in a single layer and fry for 2 to 4 minutes per side, until golden. Remove with a slotted spoon and drain on paper towels. Repeat with the rest of the falafel.

4 cups cauliflower florets

3 cloves garlic, minced

¼ cup diced onion

¼ cup fresh parsley

¼ cup fresh cilantro

2 teaspoons lemon zest

1½ ounces pork rinds, crushed in a blender (makes ¾ cup), divided (½ cup and ¼ cup)

½ tablespoon ground cumin

¾ teaspoon sea salt

¼ teaspoon cayenne pepper

2 large eggs

1 cup olive oil, or enough to fill the pan ½ inch deep

STORAGE

Refrigerate for up to 5 days.

Freeze for 3 to 6 months.

Thaw, then fry again to crisp up.

NUTRITION INFO: 316 Calories | 28.8g Fat | 6.5g Total Carbs | 2.4g Fiber | **4.1g Net Carbs** | 9.6g Protein

Nutrition info includes only the ⅔ cup oil that gets absorbed into the falafel; the rest is discarded.

Unlock this recipe in the Easy Keto App

FRIED FOODS

NUT FREE

DAIRY FREE

SESAME CHICKEN

SERVING SIZE ¾ to 1 cup of chicken, or ¼ entire recipe | **SERVES 4**

This recipe will remind you of your favorite Chinese-American takeout restaurant! Lightly breaded chicken thighs are fried to perfection and coated in a sweet, sticky sauce—without any sugar or flour.

CHICKEN

1 pound boneless skinless chicken thighs, cut into 1-inch pieces

½ teaspoon sea salt

¼ teaspoon black pepper

2 large eggs

3 ounces crushed pork rinds, crushed in a blender (makes 1½ cups)

2 tablespoons avocado oil

SAUCE

1 tablespoon avocado oil

2 cloves garlic, minced

½ cup coconut aminos

¼ cup white wine vinegar

1 tablespoon Besti Brown Monk Fruit Allulose Blend

½ tablespoon toasted sesame oil

1 tablespoon sesame seeds

STORAGE

Refrigerate for up to 5 days.

Freeze for 3 to 6 months.

1. Season the chicken with salt and pepper.

2. In a small bowl, whisk the eggs. Place the crushed pork rinds in a medium bowl.

3. Heat 2 tablespoons avocado oil in a large skillet over medium-high heat. Dip the chicken pieces in the egg, gently shake off the excess, then coat with the pork rind crumbs on all sides. (Alternatively, you can place all the chicken pieces in the egg at once, and take them out one by one to dip in the crumbs.)

4. Working in batches, place the chicken in a single layer into the pan. Cook for 3 to 5 minutes on each side, until golden and cooked through to an internal temperature of 165 degrees F.

5. Remove the chicken from the pan and cover with foil to keep warm. Repeat with the remaining chicken pieces.

6. In the same skillet, heat 1 tablespoon avocado oil over medium heat. Add the garlic and sauté for about 1 minute, until fragrant.

7. Add the coconut aminos, white wine vinegar, and Besti Brown. Use a wooden spoon to scrape any browned bits from the bottom and deglaze the pan. Bring the sauce to a gentle boil, reduce the heat, and simmer for about 20 minutes, until the volume is reduced enough that the sauce is frothy and glossy, and thinly coats the back of a spoon.

8. Remove from heat. Stir in the toasted sesame oil.

9. Return the chicken to the pan and toss to coat. Sprinkle with sesame seeds. The sauce will continue to thicken as it cools from hot to warm.

Unlock this recipe in the Easy Keto App

NUTRITION INFO: 438 Calories | 26.8g Fat | 7g Total Carbs | 0.3g Fiber | 6.7g Net Carbs | 38.3g Protein

TIPS & VARIATIONS

- If you like a little heat, add some crushed red pepper flakes or sriracha to the sauce.

- Don't like pork rinds? You can use almond flour, but the chicken will be less crispy. To make it even simpler, skip the breading and simply sauté unbreaded chicken pieces in oil.

- Reducing the sauce makes it pretty salty, so I recommend serving the sesame chicken over a neutral veggie, such as plain Cauliflower Rice (page 17) or stir-fried vegetables.

POPCORN SHRIMP

SERVING SIZE 13 to 15 shrimp, or ¼ entire recipe | SERVES 4

Popcorn shrimp are bite-size shrimp coated with breadcrumbs and Cajun seasoning. A simple swap here makes the breading keto friendly and gives us all the flavor of the traditional Southern dish, without all the carbs.

1. In a large bowl, stir together the coconut flour and Cajun seasoning.

2. Pat the shrimp dry. Add it to the flour mixture and toss to coat.

3. In a small bowl, whisk together the eggs. In a medium bowl, place the crushed pork rinds.

4. Dip each shrimp into the eggs, gently shake off the excess, then press into the pork rinds, covering all sides. Set aside on a cutting board.

5. In a large skillet, heat the avocado oil over medium heat, until shimmering. Working in batches, add the shrimp in a single layer and fry for 2 to 3 minutes per side, until golden.

3 tablespoons coconut flour

2 teaspoons Cajun seasoning

1 pound small shrimp, peeled and deveined

3 large eggs

3½ ounces pork rinds, crushed in a blender (makes 1¾ cups)

¼ cup avocado oil

STORAGE

Refrigerate for up to 4 days.

Freeze for 3 to 6 months.

Fry again to crisp up.

TIPS & VARIATIONS

• Small shrimp work best for this recipe. Look for 61/70, 51/60, or 41/50 count.

• I used my homemade Cajun seasoning recipe (**www.wholesomeyum.com/cajun-seasoning-mix-recipe**), which includes salt. If yours does not, add ¼ teaspoon of salt to the coconut flour mixture.

• Popcorn shrimp is best with dipping sauce! I recommend ranch dressing, Sugar-Free Ketchup (page 251), or sugar-free tartar sauce (**www.wholesomeyum.com/keto-tartar-sauce**).

Unlock this recipe in the Easy Keto App

NUTRITION INFO: 403 Calories | 26.4g Fat | 3.6g Total Carbs | 2.6g Fiber | **1g Net Carbs** | 36.5g Protein

SNACKS & BITES

MAPLE BACON-WRAPPED BRUSSELS SPROUTS

SERVING SIZE 3 bacon-wrapped Brussels sprouts and 1½ tablespoons dipping sauce | **SERVES 8**

Everything is better wrapped in bacon! These bacon-wrapped Brussels sprouts get a sweet, caramelized upgrade with the addition of my keto friendly maple syrup and a sweet, creamy Dijon dipping sauce. You'll love these fun and flavorful appetizers.

BACON-WRAPPED BRUSSELS SPROUTS

12 strips bacon, cut in half crosswise

¼ cup Wholesome Yum Keto Maple Syrup

⅛ teaspoon cayenne pepper

24 medium Brussels sprouts (about 1 pound 1-inch sprouts; cut any large ones in half)

DIPPING SAUCE

½ cup mayonnaise

1 tablespoon Wholesome Yum Keto Maple Syrup

½ tablespoon Dijon mustard

½ teaspoon garlic powder

⅛ teaspoon cayenne pepper, or to taste

STORAGE

Refrigerate for up to 5 days.
Freeze for 3 to 6 months.

1. Preheat the oven to 400 degrees F. Place an oven-safe rack over a baking sheet.

2. Lay out the halved bacon pieces in a single layer on a cutting board. Brush with keto maple syrup and sprinkle with cayenne pepper.

3. Flip the bacon pieces over, so that the maple syrup is on the bottom. Place a Brussels sprout at the end of a bacon slice and roll up. Place onto the rack over the baking sheet, seam side down. Repeat with the remaining Brussels sprouts. Brush remaining maple syrup over the tops of the bacon-wrapped Brussels sprouts.

4. Bake for about 25 minutes, until bacon is crispy and Brussels sprouts are tender.

5. Meanwhile, make the dipping sauce. In a small bowl, stir together the mayonnaise, maple syrup, mustard, garlic powder, and cayenne pepper until smooth.

6. Serve bacon-wrapped Brussels sprouts warm with dipping sauce.

Unlock this recipe in the Easy Keto App

NUTRITION INFO: 267 Calories | 24.3g Fat | 6.6g Total Carbs | 2.5g Fiber | **4.1g Net Carbs** | 6.5g Protein

TIPS & VARIATIONS

- If your bacon is center cut or generally on the shorter side, skewer toothpicks through the bacon and sprouts before baking to keep them intact.

- If you enjoy spicy foods, double or triple the cayenne pepper.

- You can also make this recipe with other low carb green vegetables, like bundles of green beans or asparagus. Cook times will vary depending on the veggie.

WHITE CHEDDAR CRACKERS

SERVING SIZE 9 crackers | **SERVES 4**

You need only three simple ingredients to make these crunchy cheese crackers! They remind me of a white Cheddar version of the popular cheese cracker I used to enjoy as a kid. Enjoy them as a snack on their own or use them for dipping.

1. Preheat the oven to 350 degrees F. Line a baking sheet with parchment paper.

2. Combine the Cheddar and almond flour in a food processor. Process until a crumbly dough forms.

3. Add the heavy cream. Pulse briefly, until just combined. The dough should be crumbly but stick together when pressed with your fingers.

4. Form the dough into a ball and place between 2 pieces of parchment paper. Roll out into a thin rectangle, about ⅛ inch thick. Gently peel off the top layer of parchment paper, then use a chef's knife to cut the dough into 1-inch squares and place onto the prepared baking sheet. Prick a hole in the center of each cracker with a toothpick, to prevent bubbling.

5. Bake for 6 to 8 minutes, until golden around the edges. Cool completely to crisp up.

½ cup shredded sharp white Cheddar cheese

½ cup super fine blanched almond flour

1 tablespoon heavy cream

STORAGE

Store in the pantry for up to 5 days.

Freeze for 3 to 6 months.

TIPS & VARIATIONS

• Feel free to substitute other semi-hard or semi-soft cheeses, such as traditional Cheddar, Gruyere, Gouda, or Manchego. However, you may need to adjust the amount of almond flour to achieve the same consistency.

• You can make smaller or larger crackers to your liking, but the baking time will vary depending on the size.

• Herbs and spices make a delicious addition to these crackers. Try Italian seasoning or cayenne pepper.

Unlock this recipe in the Easy Keto App

NUTRITION INFO: 150 Calories | 13g Fat | 3.3g Total Carbs | 1.5g Fiber | 1.8g Net Carbs | 6.6g Protein

CHOCOLATE PEANUT BUTTER GRANOLA BARS

SERVING SIZE 1 bar, about 4 x 1½ inches in size | **SERVES 12**

It's hard to beat the convenience of a granola bar when you're on the go or just craving a quick snack. This low carb version ticks all the boxes: The bars are sweet, chewy, crunchy, and can be taken with you just like the high carb ones. Besides, you can't go wrong with chocolate and peanut butter!

¾ cup almonds

¾ cup peanuts

¼ cup plus 2 tablespoons Besti Powdered Monk Fruit Allulose Blend

1 tablespoon golden flaxseeds

¼ teaspoon sea salt

3 tablespoons creamy peanut butter

1 large egg, whisked

¼ cup plus 2 tablespoons sugar-free dark chocolate chips, divided (¼ cup and 2 tablespoons)

STORAGE

Store in the pantry for up to 7 days.

Freeze for 3 to 6 months.

1. Preheat the oven to 350 degrees F. Line an 8 x 8-inch baking dish with parchment paper.

2. Place almonds and peanuts in a food processor. Pulse intermittently just a few times, until nuts are chopped into ¼-inch pieces. Do not overmix.

3. Transfer the nuts to a large bowl. Stir in Besti Powdered, flaxseeds, and salt.

4. In a small bowl, whisk together the peanut butter and egg. Stir the mixture into the nuts.

5. Use a spatula to fold in ¼ cup of the chocolate chips and press them into the mixture.

6. Press the mixture firmly into the lined baking dish. Press remaining 2 tablespoons of chocolate chips onto the top. Place a piece of parchment paper on top and press again to compact very tightly. Remove the top piece of parchment paper.

7. Bake for 15 to 18 minutes, until the edges turn dark golden brown.

8. Cool completely in the pan. Once cooled, lift the parchment paper out of the pan and slice into 12 bars.

Unlock this recipe in the Easy Keto App

NUTRITION INFO: 161 Calories | 13.6g Fat | 5g Total Carbs | 3g Fiber | 2g Net Carbs | 5.9g Protein

TIPS & VARIATIONS

· This recipe is naturally dairy-free as long as your chocolate chips are dairy-free, so check the ingredient list.

· Look for peanut butter that is thick and creamy, not runny, and with no sugar added in the ingredients. A thick consistency is crucial for the bars to set properly.

· This recipe is flexible as long as the ratios stay approximately the same. For example, you can replace the almonds or peanuts with any other nuts of your choice, or replace the chocolate chips with unsweetened dried blueberries or cranberries.

TIPS & VARIATIONS

- You can buy store-bought sriracha mayonnaise or make your own in just a few minutes. Get the recipe here: **www.wholesomeyum.com/ sriracha-spicy-mayo-recipe**.

- If you can't find black sesame seeds, feel free to use golden ones, or simply omit them.

- If you like additional heat, drizzle with plain sriracha sauce in addition to the sriracha mayonnaise.

- This is fully cooked sushi (no raw fish), but if you like, feel free to add some sushi-grade tuna or salmon to the center filling along with the vegetables.

BACON SUSHI

SERVING SIZE 3 pieces | **SERVES 4**

This is such a fun twist on sushi, made for bacon lovers! We're using cooked bacon for wrapping in place of seaweed, cauliflower rice bound together with cream cheese instead of traditional sticky rice, and low carb veggies in the filling. Bacon sushi makes a yummy appetizer, but the carbs are low enough that this recipe can be doubled or tripled to enjoy as a meal.

1. Preheat the oven to 400 degrees F.

2. Heat the avocado oil in a small skillet over medium-high heat. Add the cauliflower rice and sauté for 2 to 3 minutes, until crisp-tender.

3. Reduce heat to low. Add the cream cheese, stirring and pressing it into the cauliflower rice with a spatula, until the cream cheese melts and is uniformly distributed. Transfer to a bowl to cool.

4. Arrange the halved bacon slices on an oven-safe rack fitted over a baking sheet.

5. Bake the bacon in the oven for 10 to 15 minutes, until cooked through but still pliable, not crisp. Cool for 10 minutes.

6. Meanwhile, cut the cucumber and bell pepper in to thin, matchstick-size strips, 1 inch long. Cut the avocado into ¼-inch-wide strips, 1 inch long.

7. Spread 1 teaspoon of the cream cheese and cauliflower rice mixture over a slice of bacon. Place 2 to 3 pieces of cucumber, 1 to 2 pieces of bell pepper, and 1 piece of avocado at the end of the bacon slice, then roll up tightly and secure with a toothpick. Repeat with the remaining bacon.

8. Drizzle sushi with sriracha mayo and sprinkle with sesame seeds.

1 teaspoon avocado oil

3 ounces (3 tablespoons) cauliflower rice, fresh or frozen

½ ounce (1 tablespoon) cream cheese, cut into 2 to 3 small chunks

6 slices bacon, cut in half crosswise

1 ounce cucumber

¾ ounce (about ¼ large) bell pepper, any color

¼ large avocado

1 tablespoon sriracha mayonnaise

¼ teaspoon black sesame seeds

STORAGE

Refrigerate for up to 3 days.

Unlock this recipe in the Easy Keto App

SNACKS & BITES

NUTRITION INFO: 210 Calories | 19.9g Fat | 3.1g Total Carbs | 1.5g Fiber | 1.6g Net Carbs | 5.1g Protein

RASPBERRY BAKED BRIE BITES

SERVING SIZE 1 bite | **SERVES 24**

If you miss the comfort food factor of pastry-wrapped baked Brie with jam, these savory raspberry baked Brie bites are a decadent low carb replacement, in a bite-size form. You'll love the combination of creamy Brie, sweet raspberry sauce, and buttery almond crust.

7½ ounces (1¾ cups) fresh raspberries

⅓ cup Besti Powdered Monk Fruit Allulose Blend

2½ cups super fine blanched almond flour

¼ teaspoon sea salt

4 tablespoons butter, melted

1 large egg, whisked

4 ounces Brie cheese, cut into 24 (½-inch) cubes

¼ cup sliced almonds

STORAGE

Refrigerate for up to 5 days.
Freeze for 3 to 6 months.

1. Combine raspberries and Besti Powdered in a small saucepan over medium heat. Cook for 20 to 25 minutes, mashing berries with a spoon or spatula as they soften, until liquid is reduced to the consistency of slightly runny preserves. Set aside to cool until no longer hot (either warm or room temperature is fine).

2. Meanwhile, preheat the oven to 350 degrees F. Line a 24-cup mini muffin tin with parchment liners.

3. In a large bowl, mix together the almond flour and salt.

4. Stir in the melted butter and egg, until well combined. The dough should be crumbly but stick together when pressed between your fingers.

5. Press the dough into the bottom and sides of the muffin liners, using about 1 packed tablespoon for each cup, leaving space in the center.

6. Bake for 6 to 8 minutes, until crusts are just cooked through, but not browned. Cool for about 10 minutes, until warm but no longer hot.

7. Carefully remove the crusts from the mini muffin tin and transfer them to a sheet pan. Spoon a teaspoon of raspberry sauce into each. Press a piece of Brie into the sauce in each cup, then sprinkle with sliced almonds.

8. Return to the oven for about 5 minutes, until the Brie is warm and melty.

Unlock this recipe in the Easy Keto App

NUTRITION INFO: 113 Calories | 9.9g Fat | 3.8g Total Carbs | 2g Fiber | 1.8g Net Carbs | 4.1g Protein

TIPS & VARIATIONS

- You can easily cut the recipe in half if you want to make 12 bites instead of 24. To cut the egg in half, crack a whole egg, whisk, and measure out 1½ tablespoons. To halve the sweetener, use 2½ tablespoons instead of ⅓ cup.

- For a shortcut, use premade sugar-free jam or preserves instead of making the raspberry sauce from scratch. Any other jam flavor, such as strawberry or blueberry, would also be delicious.

BROWN SUGAR BACON KNOTS

SERVING SIZE 1 bacon knot | **SERVES 12**

If you like candied bacon, you'll love these brown sugar bacon knots! Besti Brown adds the flavor and sweetness of brown sugar, without the added carbs. There's also a savory version in the tips if that's your preference.

1. Preheat the oven to 400 degrees F. Place an oven-safe rack over a baking sheet.

2. Tie each slice of bacon into a loose knot, then into a loose knot again, forming a loose double knot. Place onto the rack.

3. Spoon a teaspoon of Besti Brown in the center of each bacon knot, pressing gently to help it stick. Sprinkle lightly with cayenne pepper, if using.

4. Bake for 20 to 25 minutes, until bacon knots are cooked through and edges are crispy.

12 slices bacon

¼ cup Besti Brown Monk Fruit Allulose Blend

⅛ teaspoon cayenne pepper, optional

STORAGE

Refrigerate for up to 5 days.

Freeze for 3 to 6 months.

Reheat in the oven to crisp up.

TIPS & VARIATIONS

• The timing and tying technique works best with bacon that is regular thickness. If your bacon is thick-cut, the knots may be a bit more difficult to tie and baking time will increase.

• For a savory version, replace Besti Brown and cayenne pepper with grated Parmesan cheese and garlic powder.

Unlock this recipe in the Easy Keto App

NUTRITION INFO: 92 Calories | 8.7g Fat | 0.3g Total Carbs | 0.1g Fiber | 0.2g Net Carbs | 2.8g Protein

RUTABAGA CHIPS

SERVING SIZE ½ cup of chips | **SERVES 6**

If you miss potato chips (and potatoes in general) while following a keto lifestyle, rutabagas are probably the closest replacement out there. With its starchy texture, this root vegetable is an excellent low carb potato substitute in moderation, and you can make it in every form: from baked to mashed to—yes!—even chips.

1 pound rutabagas, peeled

½ tablespoon olive oil

½ teaspoon sea salt

STORAGE

Store in the pantry for 1 to 2 weeks.

If chips get soft, crisp up again in the oven at 250 degrees F.

PREP

1. Cut the rutabagas into quarters (or eighths if they are large). Use a mandoline to slice them into 1⁄16-inch-thick pieces.

2. Place rutabaga slices into a large bowl. Add olive oil and salt, and toss by hand until evenly coated.

DEHYDRATOR METHOD (RECOMMENDED)

1. Arrange the rutabaga slices in single layers on multiple dehydrator trays.

2. Dehydrate for 8 to 12 hours, preferably rotating the rack positions every 3 to 4 hours, until chips are mostly crispy. (Check your dehydrator instructions if you have multiple settings.)

3. Allow chips to cool to fully crisp up.

OVEN METHOD

1. Preheat the oven to 250 degrees F. Place oven-safe racks on top of two baking sheets.

2. Arrange rutabaga slices in a single layer on the oven-safe racks, without overlapping.

3. Bake for 1 to 2 hours, rotating and swapping the rack positions every 30 minutes, until chips are mostly crispy. (Watch them closely in the last hour so that they don't burn.)

4. Remove chips from the oven and let them cool to fully crisp up.

Unlock this recipe in the Easy Keto App ←

NUTRITION INFO: 38 Calories | 1.3g Fat | 6.5g Total Carbs | 1.7g Fiber | 4.8g Net Carbs | 0.8g Protein

TIPS & VARIATIONS

• If you don't have a mandoline to slice the rutabagas, a slicing attachment on a food processor can also work. I wouldn't recommend using a knife; it is difficult to make the slices thin enough.

• A dehydrator works best for the most evenly cooked chips and crispiest texture, but if you don't have one, you can bake them in the oven.

• You can use the same method to make chips out of other thinly sliced vegetables, such as zucchini or radishes.

• Love flavored chips? Try spraying these lightly with avocado oil spray after cooking and cooling, then toss with powdered cheese, Italian seasoning, garlic powder, paprika, or any other seasonings you like.

FATHEAD PIROZHKI

SERVING SIZE 1 pirozhok | **SERVES 12**

Pirozhki are Russian almond-shaped hand pies stuffed with sweet or savory fillings, such as meat, cabbage, or apples. This recipe is a keto friendly rendition of the pirozhki that my grandmother used to make when I was growing up, with ground beef and hard-boiled eggs inside. They make a perfectly portable snack, appetizer, or even lunch.

DOUGH

1½ cups super fine blanched almond flour

2 large eggs

3 cups shredded mozzarella cheese

¼ teaspoon xanthan gum

FILLING

1 tablespoon olive oil

¾ cup diced onion

3 cloves garlic, minced

½ pound ground beef

½ teaspoon sea salt

¼ teaspoon black pepper

3 tablespoons fresh dill, chopped

1 large hard-boiled egg, diced, optional

STORAGE

Refrigerate for up to 5 days.

Freeze for 3 to 6 months.

DOUGH

1. In a food processor, pulse the almond flour and egg, until uniform.

2. In a medium bowl in the microwave, or a double boiler on the stove, melt the mozzarella cheese, until smooth.

3. Add the melted mozzarella to the food processor, positioning the cheese so that the blades are sticking into it. Process until a uniform dough forms, scraping the sides with a spatula if necessary.

4. Sprinkle the xanthan gum over the dough. Process until well incorporated.

5. Form the dough into a ball. Cover with plastic and refrigerate while you make the filling.

FILLING

1. Heat the olive oil in a large skillet over medium heat. Add the onion. Cook for 5 to 6 minutes, until soft and starting to brown.

2. Add the garlic. Cook for 1 to 2 minutes, until fragrant.

3. Increase heat to medium-high. Add the ground beef. Season with salt and pepper. Cook, breaking the meat apart with a spatula, for 6 to 8 minutes, until browned. Allow the filling to cool for at least 10 to 15 minutes, until it's warm but no longer hot. (It's also fine if it cools to room temperature.)

4. Stir in the dill. Gently fold in the diced hard-boiled egg, if using.

Unlock this recipe in the Easy Keto App

NUTRITION INFO: 240 Calories | 17.8g Fat | 5.1g Total Carbs | 1.8g Fiber | 3.3g Net Carbs | 16.5g Protein

VEGETARIAN OPTION

EASY KETO CARBOHOLICS' COOKBOOK

ASSEMBLY

1. Preheat the oven to 350 degrees F. Line a large baking sheet with parchment paper.

2. Place the ball of dough between 2 pieces of greased or lightly oiled parchment paper. Flatten into a disc, then roll out to ⅛-inch thickness. Carefully peel back and remove the top sheet of parchment paper.

3. Use a small bowl or knife to cut the dough into 12 circles, about 4 inches in diameter. (If you've run out of dough to cut circles from, form a ball with what is left, roll out again, and repeat to make more circles.) Place 2 tablespoons of filling in the center of each circle. Taking one of the circles, bring two sides to the center over the filling and press to seal in a line. Place, seam side down, onto the baking sheet. Repeat with remaining dough and filling.

4. Bake for about 20 minutes, until golden brown.

TIPS & VARIATIONS

- If you use a bowl to cut out the circles of dough, lightly greasing the rim can help prevent sticking.

- For a vegetarian cabbage filling, fry approximately ¾ pound shredded cabbage in olive oil, instead of the ground beef. Then fold in the hard-boiled eggs and proceed with the rest of the recipe as written.

- For sweet pirozhki, add 2 tablespoons of Besti sweetener to the dough. You can use the cooked mock apple filling from the Mock Apple Crisp recipe on page 241. You'll need about 1½ cups of cooked filling.

MACADAMIA FAT BOMBS

SERVING SIZE 1 fat bomb | **SERVES 12**

Fat bombs are little bites or snacks that are high in (at least 85%) fat and low in carbs and protein—making them ideal for fullness and maintaining an ideal macro ratio for a keto diet. This particular fat bomb recipe tastes like a fudgy blend of macadamia nut butter, cocoa butter, coconut, and vanilla.

1¼ cups macadamia nuts, divided (1 cup and ¼ cup)

2 tablespoons coconut oil, melted

½ ounce cocoa butter, melted

1 teaspoon vanilla extract

⅛ teaspoon sea salt, or to taste

3 tablespoons Besti Powdered Monk Fruit Allulose Blend, or to taste

Flaky sea salt, optional

STORAGE

Freeze for 3 to 6 months.

1. Pulse 1 cup of the macadamia nuts in a food processor or high-power blender, until mostly broken down into small pieces.

2. Add melted coconut oil, cocoa butter, vanilla extract, and salt. Continue to puree, scraping down the sides as necessary, until a smooth, runny nut butter forms.

3. Add Besti Powdered, and puree until smooth. Adjust Besti Powdered and salt to taste.

4. Line a mini muffin tin with parchment liners. Spoon the batter evenly into each liner, about halfway full.

5. Using the remaining ¼ cup of macadamia nuts, push one whole macadamia nut in the center of each fat bomb. Sprinkle with flaky sea salt, if desired.

6. Freeze for at least 1 hour, until solid. Keep frozen until ready to eat.

VARIATIONS

- **Chocolate:** Add 2 to 3 tablespoons of unsweetened cocoa powder in step 3.

- **Raspberry:** Replace the whole macadamias in step 5 with whole raspberries.

- **Maple Pecan:** Replace the vanilla extract with maple extract and swap the whole macadamias in step 5 with whole pecans.

Unlock this recipe in the Easy Keto App

NUTRITION INFO: 131 Calories | 14.1g Fat | 2g Total Carbs | 1.2g Fiber | 0.8g Net Carbs | 1.1g Protein

SWEET & SALTY TRAIL MIX

SERVING SIZE ¼ cup | **SERVES 12**

One of the struggles that carb lovers have when switching to keto is giving up the convenience of quick snacks that you can grab without having to cook. This sweet and savory trail mix takes just a few minutes to throw together, lasts a long time, and is easy to take on the go, filling that gap. And who doesn't love nuts, crunchy cheese, dried berries, and chocolate?!

1. Stir all ingredients together.

2. Store in an airtight container or glass jar.

TIPS & VARIATIONS

- Puffed cheese, not to be confused with cheese puffs, is a shelf-stable, crunchy dried cheese in the shape of small nuggets, which can be found in the snacks area at the grocery store. If you can't find it, you can omit it, or make your own using this recipe: **www.wholesomeyum.com/keto-popcorn**. You'll notice it also makes a pretty decent keto popcorn substitute!

- For a dairy-free version, replace the white chocolate chips with additional dark chocolate chips and omit the puffed cheese. Most sugar-free dark chocolate chips are dairy-free, but check the ingredients list to be sure.

- I recommend roasted, salted nuts. If your nuts are unsalted, you could spray the nuts briefly with avocado oil spray and sprinkle with sea salt.

- I used a mix of white and dark sugar-free chocolate chips, but you can use just one or the other if you like—6 tablespoons total.

- Trail mix is easy to customize! Feel free to replace the nuts with other kinds you like, or omit anything you can't find. Most dried fruit is too high in sugar for a low carb lifestyle, but unsweetened dried cranberries would work instead of dried blueberries.

½ cup macadamia nuts

½ cup almonds

½ cup pecans

⅓ cup puffed cheese

⅓ cup unsweetened coconut chips

3 tablespoons sugar-free white chocolate chips

3 tablespoons sugar-free dark chocolate chips

3 tablespoons pumpkin seeds

3 tablespoons unsweetened dried blueberries

STORAGE

Store in the pantry for 6 months.

NUTRITION INFO: 226 Calories | 19.8g Fat | 10.6g Total Carbs | 5.6g Fiber | 5g Net Carbs | 5.3g Protein

Unlock this recipe in the Easy Keto App

BREAKFAST

THE BEST KETO PANCAKES

SERVING SIZE 2 (3-inch) pancakes | **SERVES 6**

You need only a few ingredients to make these easy, fluffy keto pancakes. The combination of almond and coconut flours creates a texture that's better than using either one alone. This has been the most popular pancake recipe on the blog for years and is on regular breakfast rotation for my kids.

1 cup super fine blanched almond flour

¼ cup coconut flour

2 tablespoons Besti Monk Fruit Allulose Blend

1 teaspoon baking powder

5 large eggs

⅓ cup unsweetened almond milk

¼ cup avocado oil

½ tablespoon vanilla extract

¼ teaspoon sea salt

STORAGE

Refrigerate for up to 5 days.

Freeze for 3 to 6 months.

1. In a large bowl, whisk together all ingredients, until smooth.

2. Preheat a very lightly oiled or greased pan over medium-low to medium heat. Spoon the batter into the pan, ⅛ cup at a time, to form 3-inch circles. Cover with a lid and cook for about 1½ to 2 minutes, until bubbles start to form. Flip and cook uncovered for another 1½ to 2 minutes, until browned on the other side.

3. Repeat with the rest of the batter.

TIPS & VARIATIONS

• Almond milk can be replaced with coconut milk beverage, half-and-half, or heavy cream.

• Unlike regular pancakes made with wheat flour, these cook better and flip more easily if you cover the pan with a lid while cooking the first side. Cook uncovered after flipping.

• To measure ⅛ cup of the batter for each pancake, you can either use an ⅛ cup measuring cup or just fill a ¼ cup measuring cup halfway with 2 tablespoons of batter.

• For a traditional pancake appearance, use a nonstick pan or griddle and keep the oil in the pan very minimal.

• Try classic add-ins like blueberries or sugar-free chocolate chips, or swap the vanilla for other extracts, such as banana or maple.

• Common keto friendly pancake toppings include butter, nut butter, fresh berries, sugar-free chocolate chips, and Wholesome Yum Keto Maple Syrup, shown in the photo.

Unlock this recipe in the Easy Keto App

←

NUTRITION INFO: 268 Calories | 23g Fat | 6g Total Carbs | 3g Fiber | 3g Net Carbs | 9g Protein

EASY KETO CARBOHOLICS' COOKBOOK

NO-OATS OATMEAL

SERVING SIZE ⅔ cup | **SERVES 1**

Oats are too high in carbs to be suitable for a low carb lifestyle, but this recipe makes a hot cereal with a very similar taste and texture to real oatmeal. The basic recipe needs just five ingredients (plus salt), but there are endless variations you can make with add-ins. Try the four most popular ones I have listed below.

1. In a small saucepan, stir together the hemp hearts, flaxseed meal, chia seeds, Besti, and salt.

2. Add coconut milk and whisk until smooth.

3. Place over medium heat on the stove. Simmer for about 5 minutes, until thickened. (Alternatively, microwave for 1 to 2 minutes.) If it's too thick, thin out with more coconut milk. Adjust Besti and salt to taste, if desired.

4. Serve immediately, or mix in add-ins (see opposite page for suggestions) before serving.

¼ cup hemp hearts

1 tablespoon golden flaxseed meal

½ tablespoon chia seeds

1 tablespoon Besti Monk Fruit Allulose Blend, or to taste

1 pinch sea salt, or to taste

½ cup full-fat coconut milk

STORAGE

Refrigerate for up to 5 days.

Thin out with more coconut milk after reheating.

VARIATIONS

- **Maple Pecan:** Stir in ½ teaspoon maple extract and 2 tablespoons chopped pecans.

- **Chocolate Peanut Butter:** Stir in 1 tablespoon natural peanut butter and 1 tablespoon extra coconut milk, then simmer for another minute. Remove from heat and stir in 1 tablespoon sugar-free chocolate chips.

- **Strawberries & Cream:** Stir in 2 tablespoons finely chopped strawberries, 2 tablespoons additional coconut cream, and ½ teaspoon vanilla extract.

- **Cinnamon Roll:** Stir in ¾ teaspoon cinnamon and ½ teaspoon vanilla extract. In a small bowl, stir together 1 tablespoon Besti Powdered Monk Fruit Allulose Blend, ½ tablespoon coconut cream, and ¼ teaspoon vanilla extract. Drizzle over "oatmeal" in a swirl pattern.

NUTRITION INFO: 538 Calories | 47g Fat | 11g Total Carbs | 5.5g Fiber | 5.5g Net Carbs | 20.9g Protein

Unlock this recipe in the Easy Keto App

BREAKFAST

193

DAIRY FREE

VEGETARIAN

GRAIN-FREE CHOCOLATE GRANOLA

SERVING SIZE ¼ cup | **SERVES 20**

Granola is traditionally made with oats, which are high in carbs, but this nutty, low carb version creates crunchy chocolate clusters that are very similar in taste and texture to the real thing. Serve chocolate granola with a low carb milk, such as almond or coconut, or even watered-down heavy cream. It's also perfect for snacking or bringing along on the go.

1 cup almonds

1 cup hazelnuts

1 cup pecans

⅓ cup pumpkin seeds

⅓ cup Besti Monk Fruit Allulose Blend

3 tablespoons cocoa powder

¼ teaspoon sea salt

1 large egg white

¼ cup coconut oil, melted

1 teaspoon vanilla extract

STORAGE

Store in the pantry for 1 to 2 months.

1. Preheat the oven to 325 degrees F. Line a large baking sheet, or two small ones, with parchment paper.

2. Pulse almonds and hazelnuts in a food processor intermittently, until most of the nuts are chopped into large pieces, about ¼ to ½ of full size.

3. Add the pecans. Pulse again, stopping when the pecans are in large pieces. (Pecans are added later than almonds and hazelnuts, since they are softer.)

4. Add the pumpkin seeds, Besti, cocoa powder, and salt. Pulse just until everything is mixed well. Do not over-process! You want to have plenty of nut pieces remaining, and most of the seeds should be intact.

5. Remove the blade from the food processor. Add the egg white.

6. Whisk together the melted coconut oil and vanilla extract in a small bowl, then pour into the food processor. Stir well, until uniform and crumbly. (You can also transfer to a large bowl to mix, if you prefer.)

7. Transfer the mixture to the prepared baking sheet in a uniform layer, pressing together into a thin rectangle, about ¼ to ⅓ inch thick.

8. Bake for 15 to 18 minutes, until firm and no longer shiny.

9. Cool completely to crisp up before breaking apart into pieces.

Unlock this recipe in the Easy Keto App

NUTRITION INFO: 146 Calories | 14.2g Fat | 3.8g Total Carbs | 2.2g Fiber | 1.6g Net Carbs | 3.5g Protein

TIPS & VARIATIONS

- Feel free to use whatever nuts or seeds you have on hand—all are keto friendly, except cashews. Start with hard nuts, then add soft nuts, and finally seeds last.

- My nuts were roasted and salted, so only a little salt was sufficient. You may need more if you use raw nuts and seeds.

- The amount of Besti in this recipe makes it lightly sweet. If you want it very sweet, increase Besti to ½ cup.

- The entire recipe makes 5 cups of granola. Twenty servings is higher than most recipes in this book, but this granola stores well for weeks, making it a good candidate for a large batch.

TIPS & VARIATIONS

- For a dairy-free version, replace the heavy cream in the glaze with full-fat coconut milk.

- I prefer naturally sweetened, homemade strawberry jam. Find the recipe at: **www.wholesomeyum.com/ sugar-free-strawberry- chia-seed-jam-recipe**. (This also works with other berries, such as blueberries or raspberries.) You can also use store-bought sugar-free jam in any flavor, but these are usually made with artificial sweeteners.

STRAWBERRY TOASTER PASTRIES

SERVING SIZE 1 pastry | **SERVES 4**

Toaster pastries were a regular weekend breakfast for me growing up but are much too high in sugar for me these days. It was fun making a healthier low carb version—complete with cookie crust, strawberry filling, and sweet glaze. I hope it brings you back to childhood like it does for me.

1. In a large bowl, stir together the almond flour, Besti, baking powder, xanthan gum, and salt.

2. Add the egg and vanilla extract. Stir well, until a uniform dough forms. If it's sticky, cover with plastic and refrigerate for 30 minutes.

3. Line a baking sheet with parchment paper. Set aside.

4. Place the dough between 2 pieces of ightly oiled parchment paper. Use a rolling pin to roll out into a very thin rectangle, about ⅛ inch thick, 14 inches wide, and 8 inches tall. Cut the dough in half, making 2 rectangles. Cut one of these into 4 pastry-sized rectangles, about 3½ x 4½ inches.

5. Spread 1½ tablespoons of jam over the center of each of the 4 small rectangles, leaving a ½-inch border without filling.

6. Fold the parchment paper over so that the uncut half of the dough is laying over the filled rectangles. Seal all four edges of each pastry tightly with your fingers.

7. Cut the pastries apart at the sealed areas and use a large turner to transfer to the prepared baking sheet, 1 inch apart. If desired, use the tines of a fork to make a textured edge. (Dip the fork in water or oil between presses to prevent sticking.) Use a fork to poke holes in the top of each pastry.

8. Freeze for at least 1 hour, until solid. Toward the end of freezing time, preheat the oven to 350 degrees F.

9. Remove pastries from the freezer and immediately bake for about 15 minutes, until golden brown. Cool completely.

10. To make the glaze, whisk together Besti Powdered and heavy cream, until you get a spreadable consistency. Spread or drizzle the glaze over the cooled pastries right before serving.

NUTRITION INFO: 308 Calories | 25.7g Fat | 13.5g Total Carbs | 6.1g Fiber | 7.4g Net Carbs | 10.7g Protein

DOUGH

1½ cups super fine blanched almond flour

2 tablespoons Besti Monk Fruit Allulose Blend

1 teaspoon baking powder

⅛ teaspoon xanthan gum

1 pinch sea salt

1 large egg, whisked

½ teaspoon vanilla extract

FILLING

¼ cup plus 2 tablespoons sugar-free strawberry jam (see Tips & Variations)

GLAZE

¼ cup Besti Powdered Monk Fruit Allulose Blend

2 tablespoons heavy cream

STORAGE

Refrigerate for up to 1 week.

Freeze for 3 to 6 months.

Apply glaze fresh after reheating.

Unlock this recipe in the Easy Keto App →

BREAKFAST

197

STICKY MONKEY BREAD

SERVING SIZE ¹⁄₁₆ entire pan | **SERVES 16**

Monkey bread is a sweet, sticky cinnamon pull-apart bread that gets eaten by tearing off small pieces. This low carb rendition uses a fathead dough with yeast to give it the same chewy, bready texture and caramelized Besti sweetener to achieve the sticky coating.

DOUGH

3 cups super fine blanched almond flour

½ cup Besti Monk Fruit Allulose Blend

2 tablespoons baking powder

1 packet (2¼ teaspoons) instant yeast

1 teaspoon inulin powder

4 large eggs

2 teaspoons vanilla extract

5 cups shredded mozzarella cheese

2 ounces cream cheese, cubed

COATING

½ cup Besti Monk Fruit Allulose Blend

1 tablespoon cinnamon

TOPPING

½ cup butter

½ cup Besti Brown Monk Fruit Allulose Blend

GLAZE (OPTIONAL)

¼ cup Besti Powdered Monk Fruit Allulose Blend

2 tablespoons heavy cream

¼ teaspoon vanilla extract

STORAGE

Refrigerate for up to 5 days.
Freeze for 3 to 6 months.

1. In a food processor, process the almond flour, Besti, baking powder, yeast, inulin powder, eggs, and vanilla extract, until smooth.

2. Combine the mozzarella and cream cheese in a large bowl. Microwave for 2 to 3 minutes or heat in a double boiler on the stove, stirring halfway through and again at the end, until smooth and easy to stir.

3. Add the cheese to the food processor, positioning the cheese so that the blades are sticking into it, and process until a dough forms, scraping the sides with a spatula if necessary.

4. Form the dough into a ball, cover with plastic, and chill for about 1 hour, until no longer sticky.

5. Toward the end of chilling time, preheat the oven to 350 degrees F. Grease a bundt pan well.

6. To make the coating, combine Besti and cinnamon in a large zip-lock bag.

7. When the dough has chilled, divide it into about 40 small balls, about 1 to 2 inches in diameter. Drop about 10 balls into the bag and shake to coat. Arrange the balls at the bottom of the bundt pan so that they are touching each other. Repeat with the remaining dough balls.

8. In a small saucepan over medium-low heat, melt the butter for the topping. Add Besti Brown and stir until dissolved. Pour evenly over the dough balls.

9. Bake for 25 to 30 minutes, until the top is golden and an inserted toothpick comes out clean. Tent with foil if the top gets too dark. Cool for 10 minutes in the pan, then invert onto a plate.

10. If making the glaze: In a small bowl, whisk Besti Powdered, heavy cream, and vanilla. Drizzle over the bread.

TIPS & VARIATIONS

- Inulin powder is a prebiotic that feeds the yeast. If you can't find it, you can use regular white sugar or coconut sugar instead; the yeast will consume most of it, so the final nutrition info won't be significantly affected.

- You can make a smaller batch by cutting the recipe in half and baking it in a small loaf pan.

- If you like caramel, try replacing the glaze with Sugar-Free Caramel Sauce (page 244).

NUTRITION INFO: 303 Calories | 25.1g Fat | 7.3g Total Carbs | 2.8g Fiber | 4.5g Net Carbs | 15.3g Protein

Unlock this recipe in the Easy Keto App →

BREAKFAST

TIPS & VARIATIONS

• To get 1½ pounds peeled celery root, you'll need about 2 pounds unpeeled root, not including greens.

• Celery root is sometimes called celeriac at the grocery store. It looks like a bumpy, beige root vegetable about the size of a softball, with a leafy top that looks like parsley. You can substitute rutabagas, turnips, radishes, or cauliflower, but the cook time will vary.

• This recipe makes a light meal. To make it more filling without adding carbs, serve with additional fried eggs or sliced avocado.

BREAKFAST SAUSAGE HASH

SERVING SIZE 1 egg and ¾ cup hash | **SERVES 8**

Hash is a comforting skillet meal featuring meat, potatoes, and onions, often served with fried eggs. This recipe swaps in celery root in place of the high carb potatoes for the same comfort food factor with far fewer carbs. Not including the salt and pepper by convention, it's a five-ingredient recipe!

1. In a 12-inch cast iron skillet over medium-high heat, cook the sausage for 8 to 10 minutes, until browned.

2. Use a slotted spoon to remove the sausage to a bowl, leaving the fat in the pan. Cover the bowl to keep warm.

3. Reduce heat to medium. Add the onion and bell peppers. Sauté for 5 to 8 minutes, until onions are translucent.

4. Reduce heat to medium-low. Add the celery root. Season with salt and pepper to taste. Cook for about 20 minutes, until the celery root is tender and slightly browned. If it's soft but not yet browning, increase heat to brown as needed.

5. Stir the sausage back into the pan.

6. Use a spoon or spatula to make 4 wells in the hash. Crack an egg into each well. Cover and cook for 5 to 7 minutes, or until eggs are done to your liking.

7. Remove the eggs with about half of the hash mixture. Repeat from step 6 with 4 more wells and the remaining 4 eggs.

1 pound ground pork breakfast sausage, no sugar added

½ large onion, diced

3 large bell peppers, diced

1½ pounds peeled celery root, cut into ½-inch cubes (makes 4½ to 5 cups)

1 teaspoon sea salt

¼ teaspoon black pepper

8 large eggs

STORAGE

Refrigerate for up to 5 days.

Freeze for 3 to 6 months, without the eggs.

Unlock this recipe in the Easy Keto App

→

NUTRITION INFO: 233 Calories | 14.4g Fat | 12.4g Total Carbs | 3g Fiber | **9.4g Net Carbs** | 14g Protein

GLAZED DONUTS

SERVING SIZE 1 glazed donut | **SERVES: 6**

I've made at least half a dozen different keto donut recipes before, but this one beats them all! While most are more cake-like in texture, these glazed donuts have a light, chewy texture like a traditional glazed donut.

DONUTS

¾ cup super fine blanched almond flour

¼ cup Besti Monk Fruit Allulose Blend

3 tablespoons whey protein powder

3 tablespoons plus 1 teaspoon psyllium husk powder

1½ teaspoons baking powder

¼ teaspoon sea salt

1½ tablespoons butter, melted

2 large egg whites, at room temperature

½ teaspoon vanilla extract

¼ cup plus 2 tablespoons boiling water

GLAZE

2 tablespoons butter, melted

¼ teaspoon vanilla extract

½ cup Besti Powdered Monk Fruit Allulose Blend

1 tablespoon heavy cream

STORAGE

Refrigerate for up to 5 days.
Freeze for 3 to 6 months.

Unlock this recipe in the Easy Keto App

1. Preheat the oven to 350 degrees F. Grease a nonstick metal donut pan generously.

2. In a large bowl, stir together the almond flour, Besti, whey protein powder, psyllium husk powder, baking powder, and salt.

3. Stir in the butter, egg whites, and vanilla extract, until a uniform dough forms.

4. Pour in the boiling water while beating with a hand mixer at low speed for about 1 minute. The dough will absorb the water. Do not overmix. Let the dough sit for 5 to 10 minutes to thicken.

5. Divide the dough into 6 sections. Use oiled hands to roll a log out of the dough, place into the greased donut pan, and seal the ends to make a circle. Smooth the dough on top. Repeat with all 6 sections.

6. Bake for 15 to 18 minutes, until dark golden brown on top and an inserted toothpick comes out almost clean (not totally clean is okay). Allow donuts to cool in the pan for 15 minutes.

7. Run a small silicone spatula along the outside of the donuts and inside the donut holes. Gently slide the spatula underneath the donuts to release. Cool completely on a cooling rack or plate before glazing.

8. When the donuts have cooled, make the glaze. Melt butter in a small bowl. Stir in the vanilla extract. Add Besti Powdered and stir to form a paste. Thin out with heavy cream, until the consistency is similar to that of white school glue.

9. Dip the more rounded side of each donut (the side that was against the donut) into the glaze. (You can pour the glaze for the last donut if it becomes too shallow to dip into.)

NUTRITION INFO: 179 Calories | 14.6g Fat | 8.1g Total Carbs | 5.4g Fiber | 2.7g Net Carbs | 6.1g Protein

TIPS & VARIATIONS

- If your kitchen is warm, it may help to chill the dough for 20 minutes before rolling it into logs for the donut pan.

- For a nut-free version, swap the almond flour with sunflower seed meal.

- For a chocolate glaze, add a tablespoon of cocoa powder to the glaze, then thin out as needed with additional cream.

STRAWBERRY MILKSHAKE

SERVING SIZE 1 cup | **SERVES 4**

A milkshake is the ultimate diner treat—and sadly, it usually comes with an astounding amount of sugar. Fortunately, it's super simple to make your own low carb version. Once you have my keto friendly Easy Ice Cream (page 230 prepared in advance, this milkshake can be ready to enjoy in just a few minutes.

1. Combine strawberries, ice cream, almond milk, Besti Powdered, and vanilla extract, if using, in a blender. Blend until smooth.

2. If needed, adjust Besti Powdered to taste, or add more almond milk if the shake is too thick.

1 pound strawberries, sliced

1 recipe (3 cups) Easy Ice Cream (page 230)

⅓ cup unsweetened almond milk

⅓ cup Besti Powdered Monk Fruit Allulose Blend, or to taste, optional

1 teaspoon vanilla extract, optional

STORAGE

The milkshake is best fresh, as it will melt if not consumed right away.

TIPS & VARIATIONS

- For an even richer milkshake, replace the almond milk with heavy cream.

- Make different berry flavors by replacing the strawberries with raspberries, blueberries, or blackberries.

- For a vanilla milkshake, omit the strawberries and use ½ tablespoon of vanilla extract.

- For a chocolate milkshake, dissolve 3 to 4 tablespoons of unsweetened cocoa powder in ¼ cup of warm water. Add the chocolate mixture to the blender with the other ingredients, omitting the strawberries.

- For the complete diner experience, serve the milkshake topped with sugar-free whipped cream (make it yourself by beating heavy cream with Besti Powdered Monk Fruit Allulose Blend).

NUTRITION INFO: 326 Calories | 28.8g Fat | 11.6g Total Carbs | 2.5g Fiber | 9.1g Net Carbs | 6.3g Protein

Unlock this recipe in the Easy Keto App

BREAKFAST

CASSEROLES

SHEPHERD'S PIE

SERVING SIZE 1½ cups, or ¼ entire recipe | **SERVES 4**

Shepherd's pie is a casserole made with a rich meat sauce layer (traditionally lamb) topped with mashed potatoes. It's not normally keto friendly, since it usually contains starch in the gravy, mashed potatoes on top, and high carb vegetables like peas and carrots. Luckily, with just a few swaps we can make this dish low carb: cauliflower mash instead of potatoes, green peppers instead of peas, a smaller amount of carrots, and no starches in the sauce.

1 recipe (2 cups) Simple Mashed Cauliflower (page 77)

2 tablespoons olive oil

½ cup diced onions

½ cup diced carrots

½ cup diced green bell peppers

1 pound ground lamb

½ teaspoon sea salt

¼ teaspoon black pepper

1 cup beef bone broth

1 tablespoon coconut aminos

2 tablespoons tomato paste

½ tablespoon Italian seasoning

STORAGE

Refrigerate for up to 5 days.
Freeze for 3 to 6 months.

1. Make the mashed cauliflower according to instructions on page 77. Set aside.

2. Preheat the oven to 400 degrees F.

3. Heat olive oil in a large enameled cast iron skillet over medium heat. Add the onions, carrots, and bell peppers. Sauté for 6 to 10 minutes, until lightly browned.

4. Push the vegetables to the sides of the pan. Add the ground lamb, breaking apart with a spatula. Season with salt and pepper. Cook for 7 to 10 minutes, until the meat is browned. Stir the vegetables into the meat toward the end.

5. Stir in the beef bone broth, coconut aminos, tomato paste, and Italian seasoning. Increase heat to bring to a boil, then reduce heat and simmer, uncovered, for about 5 minutes, until most of the liquid evaporates and the sauce has thickened. Remove from heat.

6. Drop dollops of mashed cauliflower over the pan and use a rubber spatula to spread evenly across the top.

7. Bake for 10 to 15 minutes, until the edges are bubbly.

8. If desired, place under the broiler for 2 to 4 minutes, until the edges are golden.

Unlock this recipe in the Easy Keto App

NUTRITION INFO: 545 Calories | 41.7g Fat | 17.6g Total Carbs | 5.7g Fiber | 11.9g Net Carbs | 25.2g Protein

VARIATIONS

- For a dairy-free version, use the dairy-free variation of the Simple Mashed Cauliflower (see Tips & Variations on page 76).

- Shepherd's pie is traditionally made with ground lamb, but you can also swap in ground beef if that's what you have on hand.

- It's fine to substitute regular beef broth for the beef bone broth, but the meat sauce will be less flavorful.

VARIATIONS

- If you don't eat pork, use turkey bacon, or simply omit the bacon altogether for a vegetarian version.

- This casserole comes out just mildly spicy. If you enjoy more heat, double the jalapeño or top with some spicy salsa.

- For more portable individual servings, divide the mixture in a muffin tin lined with parchment paper. (Baking time will be much shorter.)

- Want to fit in more veggies? Decrease the eggs to 8 and add 1 cup of precooked low carb vegetables, such as cauliflower, broccoli, bell peppers, etc.

JALAPEÑO POPPER BREAKFAST CASSEROLE

SERVING SIZE ⅑ entire casserole | **SERVES 9**

Jalapeño poppers are a naturally low carb appetizer of halved jalapeños stuffed with cream cheese, Cheddar, and green onions and wrapped in bacon. This dish has all the same flavors in breakfast casserole form, making it an ideal complete meal for holidays, brunches, or even breakfast for dinner.

1. Preheat the oven to 350 degrees F.

2. In a large bowl, whisk together the eggs, heavy cream, salt, and pepper.

3. In the bottom of an 8 x 8-inch glass baking dish, layer about ⅔ of the bacon (8 slices, crumbled or chopped), 1 cup of the Cheddar, garlic, and minced jalapeño, in that order, trying to keep the density of each ingredient uniform. Slowly pour the egg mixture into the dish, being careful not to disturb the layers too much.

4. Bake for about 10 minutes, until eggs are starting to set around the edges but still wet in the middle.

5. Remove from the oven and drop small pieces of cream cheese evenly over the casserole. Layer the top with the remaining ½ cup of Cheddar, sliced jalapeño, and last ⅓ of the bacon (about 4 slices, crumbled or chopped).

6. Bake for 20 to 25 more minutes, until eggs are set.

7. Remove from the oven and top with green onions.

12 large eggs

½ cup heavy cream

¼ teaspoon sea salt

¼ teaspoon black pepper

12 slices cooked bacon, chopped or crumbled, divided (8 slices and 4 slices)

1½ cups shredded Cheddar cheese, divided (1 cup and ½ cup)

2 cloves garlic, minced

1 medium jalapeño, half minced and half thinly sliced

4 ounces cream cheese, cut into ½-inch chunks

1 medium green onion, green part only, sliced

STORAGE

Refrigerate for up to 5 days.

Freezing is not recommended.

NUTRITION INFO: 311 Calories | 25.8g Fat | 1.9g Total Carbs | 0.1g Fiber | **1.8g Net Carbs** | 17.5g Protein

Unlock this recipe in the Easy Keto App

CHICKEN CAESAR CASSEROLE

SERVING SIZE 1½ cups, or ⅙ entire recipe | **SERVES 6**

If you like chicken Caesar salad, you'll love this chicken Caesar casserole! Roasted spaghetti squash, tomatoes, and chicken get tossed in a creamy Caesar dressing and topped with Parmesan, for the ultimate comfort food meal that feels like you're eating pasta.

1 (3½-pound) spaghetti squash

1½ cups cherry tomatoes

2 tablespoons olive oil

¾ teaspoon sea salt, divided (¼ teaspoon and ½ teaspoon)

¼ teaspoon black pepper

2 cups cubed or shredded cooked chicken breast

2 tablespoons fresh parsley

2 cloves garlic, minced, optional

¾ cup Caesar dressing

½ cup shredded Parmesan cheese

STORAGE

Refrigerate for up to 5 days.
Freeze for 3 to 6 months.

1. Preheat the oven to 425 degrees F. Line a medium baking sheet with foil.

2. Slice the spaghetti squash in half. To make it easier, score where you're planning to cut first. Scoop out the seeds.

3. Place the spaghetti squash halves, cut side up, onto the lined baking sheet. Arrange the cherry tomatoes around the squash. Drizzle the squash and tomatoes with olive oil. Season with ¼ teaspoon of the salt and pepper. Flip the squash over so that they are cut side down.

4. Roast squash and tomatoes in the oven for 25 to 35 minutes, until a knife can be inserted into the squash skin with just a little resistance and the tomatoes burst. Remove from the oven and leave the oven on at 400 degrees F.

5. Use a fork to scrape the squash from the shells, with the tines perpendicular to the length of the squash, and release the strands into a large bowl. Add the chicken, tomatoes (but try to avoid adding any excess liquid released by the burst tomatoes), parsley, garlic, Caesar dressing, and remaining ½ teaspoon of salt.

6. Transfer the mixture into a 7 x 10-inch baking dish. Sprinkle with Parmesan.

7. Bake for about 10 minutes, until the cheese is melted.

Unlock this recipe in the Easy Keto App

NUTRITION INFO: 384 Calories | 28.5g Fat | 14.3g Total Carbs | 3.7g Fiber | **10.6g Net Carbs** | 19.9g Protein

TIPS & VARIATIONS

- This recipe starts with cooked chicken breast, and you can use any kind you have on hand. Options include rotisserie chicken, packaged precooked chicken breast, diced baked chicken breast, or shredded slow-cooked chicken breast.

- You can use premade Caesar dressing for convenience, but check labels for added sugar or artificial ingredients. You can also make homemade Caesar dressing with this recipe: **www.wholesomeyum.com/ caesar-dressing-recipe**.

- For additional veggies, try roasting broccoli florets or chopped bell peppers alongside the squash and tomatoes, or sauté a bit of spinach and stir that in at the end before baking.

TIPS & VARIATIONS

- This recipe uses precooked chicken, and you can use any kind you have on hand. Options include rotisserie chicken, packaged precooked chicken breast, diced baked chicken breast, or shredded slow-cooked chicken breast.

- The amount of salt in the recipe assumes that your shredded chicken had salt added before cooking. If it's completely unsalted, you can add more salt to taste after stirring the chicken into the sauce in step 4.

- Not a fan of pork rinds? They give a texture reminiscent of breadcrumbs on top, but feel free to omit them if you don't like them.

CHICKEN CORDON BLEU CASSEROLE

SERVING SIZE 1 cup, or ¹⁄₁₂ entire casserole | **SERVES 12**

Chicken cordon bleu is a Swiss dish (despite the French name!) of breaded chicken with ham and Swiss cheese wrapped inside. This casserole is a much easier-to-make spin on all the same flavors, with a neutral-flavored veggie (cauliflower) added to make it a full meal in one dish.

1. Preheat the oven to 400 degrees F.

2. In a large bowl, toss the cauliflower with avocado oil. Season with salt and pepper.

3. Arrange the cauliflower on a baking sheet. Roast in the oven for 25 to 30 minutes, until golden on the edges.

4. Meanwhile, in a large bowl, stir together the sour cream, heavy cream, mustard, garlic, and 1 cup of the cheese. Stir in the chicken and ham.

5. When the cauliflower is done, leave the oven on at 400 degrees F. Fold the cauliflower into the cream mixture. Adjust salt and pepper to taste, if needed.

6. Transfer the mixture to a 9 x 13-inch casserole dish. Sprinkle the remaining 1 cup of cheese over the top, followed by the pork rinds.

7. Bake for 10 minutes, until the cheese is melted. If desired, you can broil the casserole for 2 to 3 minutes to brown the topping.

1 head cauliflower, cut into florets

¼ cup avocado oil

¼ teaspoon sea salt

¼ teaspoon black pepper

1 cup sour cream

¼ cup plus 2 tablespoons heavy cream

2 tablespoons Dijon mustard

4 cloves garlic, minced

2 cups shredded Swiss cheese, divided in half

1½ pounds (2½ cups) cooked chicken, shredded

12 ounces deli ham slices, chopped

½ ounce pork rinds, crushed in a blender (makes ¼ cup), optional

STORAGE

Refrigerate for up to 5 days.

Freeze for 3 to 6 months.

NUTRITION INFO: 353 Calories | 25g Fat | 4.6g Total Carbs | 1.1g Fiber | 3.5g Net Carbs | 27.2g Protein

Unlock this recipe in the Easy Keto App

TATER TOT HOTDISH

NUT FREE

VEGETARIAN OPTION

SERVING SIZE ⅛ entire casserole | **SERVES 8**

Hotdish is a popular comfort food meal here in Minnesota, and while my Russian parents probably still have no idea what it is after 30-plus years of living here, my American best friend from my teen years frequently had this casserole at her house. My memory of her dad's hotdish centers around ground beef, frozen tater tots, green beans, corn, and canned cream of mushroom soup. After making my own keto friendly tater tots (page 86), I couldn't resist using them in a clean, low carb version of hotdish as well.

1 tablespoon avocado oil

½ large onion, diced

1 pound ground beef

1¼ teaspoons sea salt, divided (1 teaspoon and ¼ teaspoon)

½ teaspoon black pepper, divided in half

1 (14½-ounce) can green beans, drained and patted dry

1 (7-ounce) jar sliced mushrooms, drained and patted dry

½ cup sour cream

1½ cups shredded Cheddar cheese, divided (1 cup and ½ cup)

1 recipe (24 pieces) Crispy Baked Cauliflower Tots (page 86)

STORAGE

Refrigerate for up to 5 days.

Freeze for 3 to 6 months.

1. Preheat the oven to 400 degrees F.

2. Heat the avocado oil in a large skillet over medium-high heat. Add the onion and sauté for 7 to 8 minutes, until translucent and starting to brown.

3. Add the ground beef, 1 teaspoon of the salt, and ¼ teaspoon of the pepper. Cook for 7 to 10 minutes, until browned.

4. Transfer the beef mixture into a large bowl. Stir in the green beans, mushrooms, sour cream, 1 cup of the Cheddar, and the remaining ¼ teaspoons of salt and pepper (or season to taste).

5. Transfer the mixtureinto a 7 x 10-inch casserole dish. Place a single layer of cauliflower tots on top. Sprinkle with the remaining ½ cup of Cheddar.

6. Bake for 10 to 15 minutes, until the casserole is hot and the cheese is melted.

VARIATIONS

- For a vegetarian version, replace the beef with additional green beans and mushrooms, or add other veggies like cooked broccoli, bell peppers, or zucchini.

- This recipe uses canned green beans and jarred mushrooms for convenience, as this is typical of hotdish, but feel free to use fresh. Sauté them first and salt to taste before using them in the casserole.

Unlock this recipe in the Easy Keto App

NUTRITION INFO: 418 Calories | 30.1g Fat | 9.4g Total Carbs | 3.4g Fiber | 6g Net Carbs | 29.1g Protein

VEGETARIAN OPTION

CAULIFLOWER BAKED "ZITI"

SERVING SIZE 1 cup, or 1⁄12 entire casserole | **SERVES 12 SERVINGS**

Baked ziti is an Italian-American baked pasta dish with meats, marinara sauce, and cheese. This low carb version uses roasted cauliflower instead of the pasta—but with all the rich Italian flavors, you won't miss it one bit! Plus, it cooks much more quickly than the high carb pasta versions.

ROASTED CAULIFLOWER

2 heads cauliflower, cut into bite-size florets

1⁄4 cup olive oil

3⁄4 teaspoon sea salt

1⁄4 teaspoon black pepper

SAUSAGE MARINARA

1 tablespoon olive oil

1 pound ground Italian sausage

4 cloves garlic, minced

1 1⁄2 cups marinara sauce

2 teaspoons Italian seasoning

ASSEMBLY

1 1⁄2 cups whole milk ricotta cheese

1 1⁄2 cups shredded Parmesan cheese

2 1⁄2 cups shredded mozzarella cheese

STORAGE

Refrigerate for up to 5 days.

Freeze for 3 to 6 months.

1. Preheat the oven to 425 degrees F. Line 2 baking sheets with foil or parchment paper.

2. In a large bowl, toss together the cauliflower, 1⁄4 cup of the olive oil, salt, and pepper.

3. Arrange the cauliflower in a single layer on the baking sheets. Roast for about 25 minutes, until browned. (Ideally the baking sheets would fit side by side, but if not, rotate them halfway through.) When done, reduce oven temperature to 400 degrees F.

4. Meanwhile, heat 1 tablespoon of olive oil in a large skillet over medium-high heat. Add the sausage.

5. Cook, breaking apart with a spatula, for 8 to 10 minutes, until fully cooked and browned.

6. Make a well in the center and add the garlic. Sauté for about 1 minute, until fragrant, then stir into the sausage.

7. Add the marinara sauce and Italian seasoning. Simmer for 2 to 3 minutes, until the sauce is thick and bubbly. If needed, adjust salt and pepper to taste.

8. Arrange half of the cauliflower in a single layer in the bottom of a 9 x 13-inch baking dish. Dollop half of the ricotta over the cauliflower, then sprinkle with half of the Parmesan. Top with half of the sausage marinara (dollop it on, then spread), and finally sprinkle with half of the mozzarella. Repeat the layers with the remaining cauliflower, ricotta, Parmesan, sausage marinara, and mozzarella.

9. Bake in the oven for 10 to 15 minutes, until the cheese is melted and golden.

Unlock this recipe in the Easy Keto App ←

NUTRITION INFO: 381 Calories | 29.3g Fat | 10.7g Total Carbs | 2.7g Fiber | 8g Net Carbs | 19.9g Protein

VARIATIONS

- For a vegetarian version, omit the Italian sausage and make the marinara sauce meat free. You can also swap in sautéed spinach and/or mushrooms.

- Feel free to use other ground meats, such as beef, turkey, or chicken, instead of the sausage.

TIPS & VARIATIONS

- Yellow squash is sometimes called summer squash. You can also use zucchini squash.

- I highly recommend solid white albacore tuna for this recipe, as it's the best quality and will really shine in your casserole. Avoid tuna labeled "light," which has a minced consistency and a fishier flavor.

- Not a fan of pork rinds? They give a texture reminiscent of breadcrumbs on top, but feel free to omit them if you don't like them.

TUNA NOODLE CASSEROLE

SERVING SIZE 1 cup, or ⅑ entire casserole | **SERVES 9**

Tuna noodle casserole is a comforting dish featuring pasta, canned tuna, peas, a creamy sauce, and a crunchy topping like chips or breadcrumbs. My keto friendly version uses yellow squash noodles in place of pasta, bell peppers in place of peas, a clean homemade sauce, and pork rinds for the crunch on top.

1. Preheat the oven to 400 degrees F.

2. Heat 2 tablespoons of the olive oil in a 12-inch skillet over medium-high heat. Add the yellow squash and season with salt and pepper. Sauté for 3 to 5 minutes, mixing occasionally with tongs, until crisp-tender. Transfer squash noodles to a colander over the sink.

3. Add the onion to the pan and decrease heat to medium. Sauté for about 5 minutes, until translucent.

4. Add the bell pepper and garlic. Sauté for about 5 minutes, until peppers and onions are starting to brown.

5. Add the chicken broth. Use a wooden spoon to scrape the browned bits from the bottom of the pan. Increase heat to bring the liquid to a boil, then reduce heat and simmer for 3 to 5 minutes, until the liquid volume is reduced by half.

6. Reduce heat to low. Stir in the heavy cream and 1½ cups of the Parmesan, until the cheese melts and sauce is smooth.

7. Gently stir the tuna into the sauce.

8. Gently press on the noodles in the colander to drain excess water. Transfer to a 9 x 13-inch baking dish. Pour the sauce, tuna, and vegetables over the noodles and use tongs to coat.

9. In a small bowl, use a fork to mash together the remaining ⅓ cup of Parmesan, pork rinds, and remaining tablespoon of olive oil. Crumble the mixture over the casserole.

10. Bake for 10 to 15 minutes, until bubbly. Broil for 2 to 4 minutes, until the topping is golden brown.

3 tablespoons olive oil, divided (2 tablespoons and 1 tablespoon)

6 medium (4 pounds) yellow squash, spiralized and trimmed to noodle length

1 teaspoon sea salt

½ teaspoon black pepper

½ large onion, diced

1 large green bell pepper, diced

3 cloves garlic, minced

1 cup chicken broth

1½ cups heavy cream

1½ cups plus ⅓ cup grated Parmesan cheese, divided (1½ cups and ⅓ cup)

3 (5-ounce) cans solid white albacore tuna, drained

1⅓ ounces pork rinds, crushed in a blender (makes ⅔ cup)

STORAGE

Refrigerate for up to 5 days.

Freeze for 3 to 6 months.

NUTRITION INFO: 358 Calories | 26g Fat | 8.3g Total Carbs | 1.9g Fiber | 6.4g Net Carbs | 23.9g Protein

Unlock this recipe in the Easy Keto App

CLASSIC BEEF LASAGNA

SERVING SIZE: ¹⁄₁₂ entire lasagna | **SERVES 12**

This casserole has not only the classic ground beef, marinara, and gooey cheese you expect in a lasagna, but also real pasta layers that taste like the real thing. Although this lasagna takes a little effort, it's really not hard to make—and so worth it!

LASAGNA NOODLES

¾ cup lupin flour

6 large egg yolks

3 cups shredded mozzarella cheese

MEAT SAUCE

1½ pound ground beef

1 teaspoon sea salt

½ teaspoon black pepper

2 cups marinara sauce

1 tablespoon Italian seasoning

1 teaspoon garlic powder, optional

CHEESE FILLING

8 ounces whole milk ricotta cheese

½ cup grated Parmesan cheese

1 large egg

CHEESE TOPPING

2 cups shredded mozzarella cheese

STORAGE

Refrigerate for up to 5 days.
Freeze for 3 to 6 months.

LASAGNA NOODLES

1. In a food processor, process the lupin flour and eggs, until uniform, dry crumbs form.

2. In a large bowl, microwave the mozzarella for about 90 seconds, or heat in a double boiler on the stove, stirring halfway through and at the end, until smooth and easy to stir.

3. Add the cheese to the food processor, positioning the cheese so that the blades are sticking into it, and process until a dough forms. Pulse or scrape the sides as necessary.

4. Divide the dough into 2 balls. If it's sticky, cover with plastic and refrigerate for 30 minutes. Place one ball of dough between two lightly greased pieces of parchment paper and roll out into a very thin rectangle, 9 x 13 inches in size. Repeat with the other ball of dough.

MEAT SAUCE

1. Place the ground beef into a large sauté pan. Season with salt and pepper. Cook over medium-high heat for about 10 minutes, breaking apart the meat with a spatula, until browned.

2. Stir in the marinara sauce, Italian seasoning, and garlic powder, if using. Reduce heat and simmer for about 10 minutes.

CHEESE FILLING

1. While the meat sauce is simmering, make the cheese filling. In a small bowl, stir together the ricotta, Parmesan, and egg.

Unlock this recipe in the Easy Keto App

NUTRITION INFO: 438 Calories | 29.5g Fat | 8.7g Total Carbs | 3.6g Fiber | 5.1g Net Carbs | 36.5g Protein

ASSEMBLY

1. Preheat the oven to 375 degrees F.

2. Spread half of the meat sauce into the bottom of a 9 x 13-inch stoneware casserole dish. Top with one large 9 x 13-inch lasagna noodle. (To do this, peel away the top piece of parchment paper from the noodle, flip over into the baking dish, then carefully peel back the parchment paper that is now on top.) Spread half of the ricotta mixture over it, then sprinkle with half of the mozzarella. Repeat the layers of meat sauce, noodle, ricotta, and mozzarella.

3. Cover the pan with foil, not touching the cheese on top. Bake for 25 minutes. Turn the oven to broil. Remove the foil and broil for 2 to 3 minutes, until cheese is browned.

TIPS & VARIATIONS

• Lupin flour is a low carb, high-fiber flour made from lupin beans, which are part of the legume family (like peanuts). It's the key to making lasagna noodles with a texture like the real thing and can be found online.

• This base lasagna recipe is easy to customize. Feel free to swap the beef with other types of ground meat, like sausage, turkey, or chicken, or replace the marinara sauce with pesto.

CASSEROLES

DESSERTS

MINI CARAMEL CHEESECAKES

SERVING SIZE 1 mini cheesecake | **SERVES 12**

These mini cheesecakes are a single-serve version of my full-size classic cheesecake, which is the most popular dessert recipe on the blog—and for good reason: The filling is sweet, rich, creamy, and virtually indistinguishable from a regular cheesecake made with sugar. Everyone will love these!

CRUST

¼ cup plus 2 tablespoons coconut flour

½ tablespoon Besti Monk Fruit Allulose Blend

1 pinch sea salt

2 tablespoons butter, melted

1 large egg, whisked

¼ teaspoon vanilla extract

FILLING

20 ounces cream cheese, softened at room temperature

½ cup Besti Powdered Monk Fruit Allulose Blend

½ cup sour cream, at room temperature

2 teaspoons vanilla extract

1 large egg, whisked

TOPPING

¼ cup Sugar-Free Caramel Sauce (page 244)

Flaky sea salt, optional

STORAGE

Refrigerate for up to 5 days.

Freeze for 3 to 6 months.

For best results, make the caramel sauce fresh.

Unlock this recipe in the Easy Keto App

1. Preheat the oven to 350 degrees F. Line a full-size muffin tin (NOT a mini one!) with 12 silicone or parchment liners.

2. In a large bowl, stir together the coconut flour, Besti, and salt.

3. Add the melted butter, egg, and vanilla extract. Stir until crumbly, like a dry cookie dough.

4. Press the dough into the bottom of the lined muffin cups, about 2 to 3 teaspoons per cup. Bake for about 8 to 10 minutes, until golden around the edges.

5. Meanwhile, use a hand mixer or stand mixer to beat the cream cheese and Besti Powdered together at low to medium speed until fluffy.

6. Beat in the sour cream and vanilla extract. Beat in the egg.

7. Spoon the filling evenly over the crusts. Bake for 10 to 13 minutes, until the edges are set and the centers jiggle just slightly when shaking the pan. Do not wait for the filling to fully set.

8. Cool completely at room temperature, then refrigerate for at least 30 minutes, until set.

9. Spoon 1 teaspoon of caramel sauce over the center of each mini cheesecake. If desired, sprinkle with flaky sea salt.

NUTRITION INFO: 229 Calories | 21.3g Fat | 4.9g Total Carbs | 1.5g Fiber | 3.4g Net Carbs | 4.6g Protein

TIPS & VARIATIONS

- Keep the mixer at low to medium the whole time when beating the filling. High speed will introduce too many air bubbles.

- To lower the carbs even further, you can make these mini cheesecakes without the crust. Simply pour the filling directly into the liners and bake.

- Not a fan of caramel? You can serve your cheesecakes plain or topped with a berry sauce. To make it, heat berries of your choice with Besti sweetener to taste, until soft and saucy.

TIPS

- When creaming the butter and Besti, start with a lower mixer speed to prevent splattering, then increase as the ingredients are incorporated.

- If you don't have Besti Brown sweetener, you can use regular Besti and add a teaspoon of blackstrap molasses to achieve that brown sugar flavor.

- You can make the cookies thicker or thinner to your liking. Keep in mind they spread only a little, so flatten them to the thickness you want before you bake them.

CHEWY CHOCOLATE CHIP COOKIES

SERVING SIZE 1 cookie | **SERVES 22**

These soft and chewy chocolate chip cookies are perfect with a cold glass of almond or coconut milk. You only need a few ingredients and about 20 minutes to make them, so they're a great quick dessert to satisfy those cookie cravings.

1. Preheat the oven to 350 degrees F. Line a baking sheet with parchment paper.

2. Use a hand mixer or stand mixer to beat together the butter and Besti Brown, until fluffy.

3. Beat in the egg and vanilla extract.

4. Beat in the almond flour, ½ cup at a time. Beat in the salt.

5. Sprinkle (don't dump) xanthan gum over the cookie dough, then beat.

6. Fold in the chocolate chips.

7. Use a medium cookie scoop (1½ to 2 tablespoons in size) to scoop rounded portions of the dough, pack tightly, then release onto the prepared baking sheet. Use your palm to flatten each cookie to about ⅓ inch thick.

8. Bake for 10 to 14 minutes, until the edges are golden. (Time will vary depending on your oven and the thickness of your cookies.) Allow to cool completely on the pan before handling.

½ cup butter, softened

⅓ cup Besti Brown Monk Fruit Allulose Blend

1 large egg, at room temperature

½ tablespoon vanilla extract

2¾ cups super fine blanched almond flour

½ teaspoon sea salt

½ teaspoon xanthan gum

½ cup sugar-free dark chocolate chips

STORAGE

Store in the pantry for up to 3 days.

Refrigerate for up to 1 week.

Freeze for 3 to 6 months.

NUTRITION INFO: 134 Calories | 12.6g Fat | 4.6g Total Carbs | 2.6g Fiber | **2g Net Carbs** | 3.9g Protein

Unlock this recipe in the Easy Keto App

DESSERTS

EASY ICE CREAM

SERVING SIZE ½ cup | **SERVES 6**

This is the best ice cream I've ever made! It's easy to prepare, needs just five basic ingredients (plus salt), and comes out perfectly sweet, creamy, and scoopable. It's also the ideal base recipe for any ice cream flavor you like—see Tips & Variations on the opposite page for ideas.

5 large egg yolks

½ cup Besti Powdered Monk Fruit Allulose Blend

1 pinch sea salt

1½ cups unsweetened vanilla almond milk

1 cup heavy cream

1 teaspoon vanilla extract

STORAGE

Freeze for 3 to 6 months.

1. Freeze an ice cream maker bowl for at least 24 hours before you begin this recipe.

2. In a medium bowl, whisk together the egg yolks, Besti Powdered, and salt, until combined and light yellow in color. Set aside.

3. In a small saucepan, whisk together the almond milk and cream. Place over medium heat, until it just starts to simmer. Remove from heat.

4. Very slowly, pour the hot cream mixture into the egg yolk mixture while whisking constantly. (Pouring the hot mixture in a thin stream and whisking vigorously will prevent scrambling the egg.)

5. Once the custard is combined and smooth, transfer it mixture back to the saucepan. Place over low heat and stir frequently until the mixture reaches 170 degrees F, about 3 to 5 minutes.

6. Remove from heat. Stir in vanilla extract. Cover and refrigerate for at least 4 hours, until very cold, no more than 40 degrees F.

7. Pour the cold custard mixture into the prefrozen ice cream maker bowl. Churn according to the manufacturer's instructions, usually about 20 to 25 minutes, to a soft-serve consistency.

8. Serve immediately, or for firmer ice cream, transfer it to a freezer container and freeze until solid.

Unlock this recipe in the Easy Keto App

NUTRITION INFO: 189 Calories | 18.8g Fat | 1.8g Total Carbs | 0.1g Fiber | 1.7g Net Carbs | 3.6g Protein

TIPS & VARIATIONS

- **Chocolate ice cream:** Add ¼ cup cocoa powder to the milk and cream in step 2 before heating.

- **Strawberry ice cream:** Simmer 2 cups chopped fresh strawberries with ¼ cup Besti Powdered on the stovetop for about 5 minutes, until soft. Mash to your desired consistency, then stir into the custard after step 4.

- For a nut-free version, replace the almond milk with unsweetened coconut milk beverage (the liquid kind in a carton).

- For a dairy-free version, replace the heavy cream with full-fat canned coconut milk.

- Besti sweetener is important to use in this recipe, because it dissolves well and creates soft, scoopable ice cream. Many sugar substitutes make ice cream too icy.

SALTED PECAN PIE BARS

SERVING SIZE 1 bar, or ¹⁄₁₆ entire pan | **SERVES 16**

If you like pecan pie, you're going to love these pecan pie bars! They have a buttery shortbread crust and gooey caramel pecan topping, like a pecan pie in a perfectly portioned bar form. Plus, they come together much faster than a full-size pie.

1. Preheat the oven to 350 degrees F. Line a 9 x 9-inch metal baking dish with parchment paper, with extra hanging over the sides for easy removal later.

2. In a large bowl, stir together the almond flour, Besti, and salt.

3. In a small bowl, stir together the butter and vanilla extract. Add to the flour mixture and stir to form a crumbly dough.

4. Press the dough into the lined pan. Bake for 8 to 10 minutes, until set and golden around the edges. Cool for at least 15 minutes.

5. Meanwhile, stir ½ cup of the pecans into the caramel sauce.

6. Pour the caramel-pecan mixture over the crust and spread evenly. Sprinkle remaining ½ cup of pecans over the filling.

7. Bake for about 15 to 20 minutes, until the filling is very bubbly and darkened in color.

8. Let cool completely. Once cool, sprinkle with flaky sea salt. Lift out of the pan using the edges of the parchment paper, then slice into bars using a large chef's knife.

CRUST

2 cups super fine blanched almond flour

2 tablespoon Besti Monk Fruit Allulose Blend

¼ teaspoon sea salt

6 tablespoons butter, melted

1 teaspoon vanilla extract

TOPPING

1 cup Sugar-Free Caramel Sauce (page 224)

1 cup coarsely chopped pecans, divided in half

¾ teaspoon flaky sea salt

STORAGE

Store in the pantry for up to 2 days.

Refrigerate for up to 1 week.

Freeze for 3 to 6 months.

TIPS & VARIATIONS

• For a dairy-free version, replace the butter in the crust with unrefined coconut oil. See the Tips & Variations for Sugar-Free Caramel Sauce (page 244) on how to make the caramel dairy-free as well.

• The Sugar-Free Caramel Sauce on page 244 makes ¾ cup, so make a double batch to have enough for the 1 cup that these bars require.

NUTRITION INFO: 256 Calories | 26.1g Fat | 4.4g Total Carbs | 2.3g Fiber | 2.1g Net Carbs | 4.1g Protein

Unlock this recipe in the Easy Keto App →

DESSERTS

SIMPLE CHOCOLATE FUDGE

SERVING SIZE 1½-inch square | **SERVES 36**

If you've ever made classic fudge with condensed milk, this recipe is just like that, except we're using a homemade Sugar-Free Sweetened Condensed Milk (page 247) and sugar-free chocolate. I recommend a blend of milk and dark chocolate chips, as the fudge turns out quite dark and bitter using dark chocolate alone.

1 recipe (1½ cups) Sugar-Free Sweetened Condensed Milk (page 247)

1 cup sugar-free dark chocolate chips

1 cup sugar-free milk chocolate chips

2 tablespoons butter

½ tablespoon vanilla extract

1 pinch sea salt

STORAGE

Refrigerate for up to 1 week.
Freeze for 3 to 6 months.

1. Line a 9 x 9-inch pan with parchment paper, with the paper going up all four sides.

2. In a double boiler on the stove over medium-low heat, or in the microwave, heat the condensed milk, dark and milk chocolate chips, and butter, stirring occasionally, until smooth.

3. Remove from heat. Stir in the vanilla extract and salt.

4. Pour the mixture into the lined pan. Refrigerate for at least 2 hours, or until firm.

5. When the fudge is cold and set, use the edges of the parchment to lift it from the pan. Slice into 36 pieces. Store in the refrigerator until ready to serve, or freeze for firmer fudge.

VARIATIONS

- **White chocolate:** Replace all the chocolate chips with 2 cups of sugar-free white chocolate chips.

- **Milk chocolate:** Omit the dark chocolate chips and replace with an extra cup of milk chocolate chips.

- **Nuts:** Stir ¾ cup chopped nuts (such as walnuts, pecans, or hazelnuts) into the chocolate before pouring into the pan.

- **Peppermint:** Stir in a teaspoon of peppermint extract instead of the vanilla.

- **Layered:** Heat half of the condensed milk and butter with ½ cup each of milk and dark chocolate chips. Stir in ¾ teaspoon of vanilla extract. Pour into the pan and chill for 10 to 20 minutes. Heat the other half of the condensed milk and butter with 1 cup white chocolate chips. Stir in ¾ teaspoon of vanilla extract. Pour the white chocolate layer over the dark chocolate layer and chill again until set.

Unlock this recipe in the Easy Keto App ←

NUTRITION INFO: 102 Calories | 9.7g Fat | 2.7g Total Carbs | 2g Fiber | 0.7g Net Carbs | 0.7g Protein

TIPS & VARIATIONS

- For a dairy-free version, replace the butter with unrefined coconut oil. Butter-flavored coconut oil is even better if you can find it.

- If you prefer glazed cookies, simply whisk together ¼ cup Besti Powdered sweetener with 1 tablespoon heavy cream. Thin out with more cream, if needed, and drizzle over the top of the cooled cookies.

MOCK OATMEAL COOKIES

SERVING SIZE 1 (2-inch) cookie | **SERVES 12**

Oatmeal cookies were my absolute favorite cookie as a kid—sweet, buttery, and chewy, with a hint of brown sugar flavor—and more recently, one of the most challenging sweets to make low carb. Oats are completely off the table on a keto lifestyle, but I'm pleased to say that these mock oatmeal cookies come surprisingly close to the original, thanks to the oat fiber that adds oat flavor without carbs, Besti Brown sweetener that replaces brown sugar, and hemp seeds to mimic the texture of oats.

1. Preheat the oven to 350 degrees F. Line a baking sheet with parchment paper or a silicone mat.

2. In a large bowl, use a hand mixer to beat the butter and Besti Brown, until fluffy.

3. Beat in the egg and vanilla extract.

4. Beat in the almond flour, oat fiber, baking powder, cinnamon, and salt, until well combined.

5. For chewy cookies, sprinkle (don't dump) xanthan gum evenly over the cookie dough, then beat in using the hand mixer.

6. Stir in the hemp hearts.

7. Use a medium cookie scoop (1½ to 2 tablespoons in size) to scoop the cookie dough onto the prepared baking sheet, approximately 2 inches apart. Use a fork to flatten the cookies to about ¼- to ⅓-inch thickness, pressing the fork down in different directions to leave the surface uneven.

8. Bake for 12 to 15 minutes, until cookies are barely set and edges are golden. Cool completely before moving.

6 tablespoons butter, softened

6 tablespoons Besti Brown Monk Fruit Allulose Blend

1 large egg, at room temperature

½ teaspoon vanilla extract

¾ cup super fine blanched almond flour

¼ cup oat fiber

½ teaspoon baking powder

½ teaspoon cinnamon

¼ teaspoon sea salt

¼ teaspoon xanthan gum, optional (for chewy cookies)

¼ cup hemp hearts

STORAGE

Store in the pantry for up to 3 days.

Refrigerate for up to 1 week.

Freeze for 3 to 6 months.

Unlock this recipe in the Easy Keto App

→

NUTRITION INFO: 122 Calories | 11.6g Fat | 6g Total Carbs | 3.9g Fiber | **2.1g Net Carbs** | 3.6g Protein

DESSERTS

CLOUD CREAM PUFFS

SERVING SIZE 1 cream puff | **SERVES 12**

Cream puffs are a French dessert featuring puffy choux pastry and sweet cream filling. The real thing is pretty much a ball of sugar, but this low carb version has similar features at less than one net carb each. If you've ever made cloud bread before, these cream puffs are based on that—and if you haven't, don't worry, they are easy!

PASTRIES

2 large eggs, at room temperature, whites and yolks separated

⅛ teaspoon cream of tartar

2 ounces cream cheese, softened at room temperature

3 tablespoons Besti Monk Fruit Allulose Blend

¾ teaspoon vanilla extract

⅛ teaspoon sea salt

FILLING

¾ cup heavy cream, cold

¼ cup Besti Powdered Monk Fruit Allulose Blend

¾ teaspoon vanilla extract

STORAGE

Refrigerate pastries for up to 5 days.

For best results, make the filling fresh.

1. Preheat the oven to 300 degrees F. Line a large baking sheet with parchment paper.

2. In a large bowl, use an electric hand or stand mixer with a whisk attachment to beat the egg whites and cream of tartar until stiff peaks form.

3. In a second large bowl, use the mixer to beat the cream cheese, until fluffy. At high speed, beat in the egg yolks, Besti, vanilla extract, and salt, until smooth.

4. Using a large spatula, gradually fold the egg whites into the cream cheese mixture to gently incorporate them without breaking down their air bubbles.

5. Scoop the mixture into 24 1½-inch circles (about 1 tablespoon each) on the parchment paper, at least 1 inch apart. Bake for about 15 minutes, until golden. Remove from the oven and cool completely on the baking sheet.

6. Meanwhile, combine the heavy cream, Besti Powdered, and vanilla extract in a large bowl. Beat with a hand mixer fitted with a whisk attachment for 2 to 4 minutes, until stiff peaks form. Transfer the cream to a piping bag fitted with an open star tip.

7. When the pastries have cooled, release them by sliding a thin turner or spatula underneath each pastry. Top half the pastries with about 2 tablespoons of piped whipped cream each. Top with the remaining half of the pastries.

Unlock this recipe in the Easy Keto App

NUTRITION INFO: 81 Calories | 7.8g Fat | 0.7g Total Carbs | 0.1g Fiber | 0.6g Net Carbs | 1.7g Protein

TIPS & VARIATIONS

- If your cream cheese is too cold, you'll end up with chunks in the egg yolk mixture. If this happens, let the mixture sit for a while to soften, and then beat again until smooth.

- Unlike the cream cheese, the heavy cream in this recipe has to be cold. This makes it easier to form stiff peaks when whipping.

- Humidity can affect whipped egg whites. Your cream puffs will be delicious either way, but may be less fluffy if your environment is humid.

- For a classic cream puff look, dust your puffs with Besti Powdered sweetener and serve with strawberries. A drizzle of melted sugar-free chocolate over them is also delicious!

TIPS & VARIATIONS

- For a dairy-free version, swap the butter with unrefined coconut oil.

- The ultimate pairing for Mock Apple Crisp is my keto friendly Easy Ice Cream (page 230)!

- The time to cook the filling can vary widely, depending on the size of your zucchini pieces, your stove, and pan size and material. On average, 30 to 60 minutes is a good estimate in a large Dutch oven, but cook as long as needed to reduce the filling.

MOCK APPLE CRISP

SERVING SIZE ⅛ entire pan | **SERVES 8**

The apples, oats, and sugar found in traditional apple crisp recipes may be too high in carbs, but with a secret-ingredient filling and a nutty topping, we can still make keto friendly apple crisp! If you're skeptical that zucchini could possibly taste like apples, I promise you'll change your mind once you try this recipe.

1. In a small bowl, whisk the gelatin powder with 3 tablespoons of the lemon juice. Set aside to bloom.

2. In a Dutch oven over medium heat, melt the butter. Stir in the Besti Brown, the remaining 3 tablespoons of lemon juice, and the cinnamon, nutmeg, cardamom, and salt.

3. When the gelatin mixture has thickened, add it to the butter mixture and whisk, until dissolved.

4. Add the diced zucchini. Bring to a gentle boil, then simmer for about 30 to 60 minutes, until the squash is very soft, most of the moisture has evaporated, and the sauce starts to thicken, similar to apple pie filling. Stir in the vanilla extract, if using.

5. While the filling is simmering, make the topping. Combine the almonds, Besti Brown, butter, vanilla extract, cinnamon, and salt in a food processor. Pulse intermittently, until a coarsely textured meal forms, with some almond pieces for crunch.

6. When the filling is almost ready, preheat the oven to 350 degrees F.

7. Transfer the filling to an 8 x 12-inch oval or 9 x 9-inch square baking dish.

8. Crumble the almond topping over the filling. Bake for about 20 minutes, until the filling is bubbly around the edges and the topping is golden brown.

FILLING

1 tablespoon unflavored gelatin powder

6 tablespoons lemon juice, divided in half

½ cup butter

½ cup Besti Brown Monk Fruit Allulose Blend

2 teaspoons cinnamon

1 teaspoon nutmeg

½ teaspoon cardamom

⅜ teaspoon sea salt

5 medium zucchini, peeled, sliced and diced into ½-inch pieces, about 6 to 7 cups

1 teaspoon vanilla extract, optional

TOPPING

1½ cups almonds

¼ cup Besti Brown Monk Fruit Allulose Blend

3 tablespoons butter, melted

1 teaspoon vanilla extract

½ teaspoon cinnamon

¼ teaspoon sea salt

STORAGE

Refrigerate for up to 4 days.

Freeze for 3 to 6 months.

Unlock this recipe in the Easy Keto App

NUTRITION INFO: 326 Calories | 29.5g Fat | 11.2g Total Carbs | 5g Fiber | 6.2g Net Carbs | 8.2g Protein

SAUCES & CONDIMENTS

NUT FREE

VEGETARIAN

SUGAR-FREE CARAMEL SAUCE

SERVING SIZE 1 tablespoon | **SERVES 12**

Sweet, gooey, and packed with flavor, this sugar-free caramel sauce tastes just like the real thing. Drizzle it on all your favorite keto friendly desserts to take them up a notch!

⅓ cup salted butter

3 tablespoons Besti Brown Monk Fruit Allulose Blend

⅔ cup heavy cream

1 teaspoon vanilla extract

STORAGE

Refrigerate for up to 1 week.

Reheat in a double boiler on the stove.

1. Melt the butter and Besti Brown together in a large saucepan over low heat. Once melted, cook for about 3 to 4 more minutes, stirring occasionally, until color turns more golden brown. (Watch it carefully to avoid burning.)

2. Stir in the cream. Bring to a gentle boil, then reduce heat and simmer for 7 to 10 minutes, continuing to stir occasionally, until the mixture is a dark caramel color and coats the back of a spoon.

3. Remove from heat. Whisk in the vanilla extract.

TIPS & VARIATIONS

• The size of your saucepan has a big impact on the time it takes for caramel to thicken; it may take much longer with a small pan, sometimes over 30 minutes, so use the largest saucepan possible. If you double or triple the recipe, you may want to use a sauté pan instead.

• Besti Brown sweetener imparts the best flavor in caramel sauce, but you can also make it with the regular white sweetener version. Be sure to use an allulose-based sweetener like Besti for a smooth, gooey result that won't crystallize or have an aftertaste.

• If your caramel sauce cools and you need to reheat it, be sure to do so only in a double boiler. It may separate if you reheat directly on the stovetop or in the microwave.

Unlock this recipe in the Easy Keto App

NUTRITION INFO: 91 Calories | 9.9g Fat | 0.4g Total Carbs | 0.1g Fiber | 0.3g Net Carbs | 0.4g Protein

SUGAR-FREE SWEETENED CONDENSED MILK

SERVING SIZE 2 tablespoons | SERVES 12

I have a confession to make: I used to eat sweetened condensed milk with a spoon as a kid. Anyone else? Even if you're not as much of a die-hard fan as I am, sweetened condensed milk is a useful ingredient to have for recipes—and fortunately, it's surprisingly easy to make a sugar-free version! All you need are three simple ingredients and a little patience to let the milk thicken.

1. Melt the butter in a large saucepan over medium heat.

2. Add the heavy cream and Besti Powdered.

3. Bring to a boil, then reduce heat and simmer for 25 to 45 minutes, stirring occasionally, until the mixture coats the back of a spoon and volume is reduced by half. Avoid scraping the sides of the pan.

4. Condensed milk will thicken further as it cools.

3 tablespoons butter

2 cups heavy cream

⅓ cup Besti Powdered Monk Fruit Allulose Blend

STORAGE

Refrigerate for up to 1 week.

Condensed milk may solidify in the fridge, but will become runny again when it comes to room temperature.

TIPS

• The cook time can vary widely depending on your stove and the size and material of your pan. Larger pans will cook the condensed milk more quickly; you can even use a skillet to speed up the process.

• If you overcook the condensed milk, it will turn golden, thicken too much, and start to resemble caramel sauce. If you catch this happening before it turns too dark, you can add more cream to thin it out and lighten it. Add more Besti to taste, if needed, as well.

• Besti sweetener is important to use in this recipe, because unlike most sugar substitutes, it dissolves well and won't crystallize after it cools. This is crucial to avoid a gritty texture in your condensed milk.

NUTRITION INFO: 161 Calories | 17.2g Fat | 1.1g Total Carbs | 0.1g Fiber | 1g Net Carbs | 1.1g Protein

Unlock this recipe in the Easy Keto App

ALFREDO SAUCE

SERVING SIZE ¼ cup | **SERVES 6**

Classic Alfredo sauce is often made with a roux, which adds unnecessary carbs—and there's no reason for it, because grated Parmesan cheese does a perfectly fine job of thickening an Alfredo sauce all on its own. This recipe uses simple ingredients to create the classic, creamy sauce everyone loves.

1 tablespoon butter

6 cloves garlic, minced

1½ cup heavy cream

½ cup grated Parmesan cheese

¼ teaspoon sea salt, or to taste

¼ teaspoon black pepper, or to taste

1 pinch nutmeg, or to taste, optional

STORAGE

Refrigerate for up to 5 days.

Freeze for 3 to 6 months.

Reheat gently while stirring to avoid separation.

1. In a medium saucepan over medium heat, melt the butter. Add garlic and sauté for about 1 minute, until fragrant.

2. Add the heavy cream. Bring to a gentle simmer, then continue to simmer for about 5 minutes, stirring occasionally, until it begins to thicken and volume is reduced by about ⅓. (Amount of time will vary, depending on the size of your saucepan.)

3. Reduce heat to low. Gradually whisk in the Parmesan. Keep whisking over low heat, until smooth. Season to taste with salt, pepper, and nutmeg, if using.

TIPS

• If the sauce is thicker than you'd like, you can thin it out with more cream at the end.

• Alfredo sauce is obviously a classic over pasta (try Spaghetti Squash Alfredo on page 109 or serve over 3-Ingredient Egg Noodles on page 114), but you can also use it for Chicken Crust Pizza (page 91) or White Pizza Pockets (page 101).

Unlock this recipe in the Easy Keto App

⟵

NUTRITION INFO: 253 Calories | 25g Fat | 3g Total Carbs | 0g Fiber | **3g Net Carbs** | 3g Protein

SUGAR-FREE KETCHUP

SERVING SIZE 1 tablespoon | **SERVES 12**

There are so many meals that would be incomplete without a good dose of ketchup, but sadly, most store-bought varieties are loaded with sugar or even corn syrup. The good news is that it's actually super easy to make your own ketchup at home, without all the sugar!

1. In a small saucepan, whisk together all ingredients, until smooth.

2. Cover and simmer for about 30 minutes over low heat, stirring occasionally, until the ketchup thickens to your desired consistency. (Time will vary widely depending on the size of your pan.)

3. Adjust salt and Besti to taste, if needed.

4. For the smoothest texture, puree the ketchup in a high-power blender for at least 30 seconds, until smooth.

6 ounces tomato paste

1 cup water

¼ cup Besti Powdered Monk Fruit Allulose Blend

3 tablespoons white vinegar, or apple cider vinegar

1 teaspoon sea salt

¾ teaspoon onion powder

½ teaspoon garlic powder

¼ teaspoon paprika

⅛ teaspoon ground cloves

⅛ teaspoon mustard powder

TIPS

• The cook time can vary widely depending on your stove and the size and material of your pan. Larger pans will cook the ketchup more quickly; you can even use a skillet to speed up the process.

• Besti sweetener is important to use in this recipe, because unlike most sugar substitutes, it dissolves well and won't crystallize after it cools. This is crucial to avoid a gritty texture in your ketchup.

• Use Sugar-Free Ketchup for dipping Crispy Baked Cauliflower Tots (page 86), Popcorn Shrimp (page 165), or Rutabaga Fries (page 66). You can even use it to make burger sauce for Bacon Cheeseburgers (page 59).

NUTRITION INFO: 13 Calories | 0g Fat | 2g Total Carbs | 0g Fiber | 2g Net Carbs | 0g Protein

Unlock this recipe in the Easy Keto App →

ACKNOWLEDGMENTS

To my readers: From the bottom of my heart, thank you for being here—visiting my website, making my recipes, watching my videos, supporting my books and products, sharing your triumphs and tribulations with me, and being part of the Wholesome Yum community. The little blog that started as a hobby has completely transformed my life, and I can only hope that I can touch your lives in some way that makes a difference, too. None of this would be possible without YOU.

To my husband, Oleg: You are my rock and my best friend. I still remember when you told me "you never work with your spouse", in passing, sometime not long after we met. And yet, here we are, working together to build as many things as we can, as quickly as we can, and loving every minute of it. Thank you for supporting me, understanding me, and juggling all the moving pieces of Wholesome Yum with me. I love you to the moon and back.

To my little girls, Bella and Gaby: You bring so much joy to my life. Thank you for taste testing almost every recipe in this book, and for pushing me to make them better. No one is a tougher critic of low carb recipes than a child. If these dishes are good enough to get your seal of approval, they are good enough for my readers.

To my mom and dad: Thank you for your support and patience through the many ups and downs I went through before ending up here, and for respecting what my career has turned into, even if it's what you least expected. Most importantly, thank you for making me feel unconditionally loved.

To my photo editor (and wearer of 500 other hats), Lesley Dykes: You nailed my unique photo editing style, and I am honored to have had you edit all the photos in this book as well as help me proofread. Thank you for doing exceptional work, staying on top of everything, and being patient as I throw things at you at a moment's notice.

To my marketing manager (and wearer of 500 more hats), Amanda Suazo: Thank you for your hard work on so many pieces necessary to share my book with the world and for your patience with my incessant requests. You are an incredible writer and marketer, and you always get the Wholesome Yum voice just right.

To my culinary assistant, Sue Hall: You were indispensable in the creation of this book. Thank you for your meticulous notetaking, your helpful suggestions for improving the recipes, your attention to detail during photo shoots, and your flexibility with my crazy schedule. Cooking with you is a joy.

To the Wholesome Yum Team, past and present: Kelley, Devyn, Emily, Melissa, Jade, Natalie, Chantal, and Travis—thank you for helping to shape Wholesome Yum into what it is today.

To my product business partner, Jeff Lager: Thank you for joining me on this amazing journey to make Wholesome Yum food products a reality! It feels surreal to be using them in my second cookbook.

To my designer, LeAnna Weller Smith: You've made my dream self-published book a reality. Working with you has been seamless, organized, and everything I'd hoped it would be. Thank you for the beautiful designs (you absolutely nailed my brand style), for your patience with my very particular change requests, and for keeping everything moving on schedule.

To my editor, Samantha Holtgrewe: You have been a joy to work with and made the editing process as stress-free as possible. Thank you for your meticulous attention to detail, consistency with my brand, and excellent ideas for making the book even better.

To my distributor, Jennifer Dolce: Thank you for giving me peace of mind, being so easy to work with, and answering my endless questions. I am so grateful and delighted that my self-published book will be available through most of the traditional channels.

To my recipe testers: I was completely overwhelmed and humbled by the number of applicants to test this book's recipes. I am so grateful for each and every one. Below is the list of Wholesome Yum readers that made at least one recipe in this cookbook and submitted feedback. Thank you for helping make my recipes better, clearer, and easier.

Abby Myers
Allison Burke
Amanda Riley
Amber Herrick
Amelia Fuentes
Amy Buijze
Amy Lara
Anita Soike
Anna Churgai
Annette Strenge
Annie Coady
Ashlee Altman
Ashley Wells
Barbara Brown
Barbi Schoppert
Becky Brundage
Beth Corrente
Betsy Grugin
Beverly Appler
Brandi Villegas
Brenda Campagna
Brianne Lawton
Carol Mangles
Carrie Logan
Cathy Kelley
Celeste Boggs
Charlotte Locey
Christi MacMillin
Christine Lodge
Cindy Gamble
Constance Terry
Dana Duxbury
David Chapdelaine
David Dyjak
Debbie Gagnon
Debbie Henry

Debbie Kafford
Debbie Sabadin
Deborah Sanford
Denita Mora
Diana Polnaszek
Donna Shields
Eileen Mishler
Elizabeth Hill
Eva Baker
Genna Watkins
Gina Rallo
Glenda Ward
Jaime Golobish
Jamie Germain
Jane Sumner
Janet Ball
Jenna Harper
Jennifer Dages
Jennifer Lopez
Jordan Crane
Joyce Kostro
Joyce Row
Julie Degen
Justin Lanners
Kassi Seefeldt
Kathleen Coupe
Kathryn Petro
Kathy Binfet
Kathy Daugherty
Kelly Brown
Keri Blankenship
Kim Kelly
Kim Magee
Kimberlee Abels
Krista Turner
Kristen Gilmartin

Krystal Ruhl
Laura Samuelson
Laura Wisser
Lauren Ruch
Laurie DePauw
Laurie Vowell
Lin Nelson-Mayson
Lisa Goossen
Lisa Monday
Lisa O'Bryan
Lisa Thomas
Lynda Pedersen
Marie Striker
Marriah Smith
Marva Osborn
Mary Hovda
Mary Miller
Mary Screws
Matthew Barnett
Maureen Vieth
Melanie Rager
Melinda Yeager
Melissa Brown
Melissa Terrell
Melissa Visconti
Melony Vance
Michele P.
Mickey Buehler
Naomi Burgos
Natalie Payton
Nedda Schoenfeld
NJ Miler
Pat Quinsey
Patricia Kovalski
Paul Wilder
Paula Boedigheimer

Paula Zarlenga
Peter Schott
Ponarett Xieng
Rebecca Sauve
Renee Roberson
Rhonda Marcinko
Roberta Hasstedt
Robin Brawner
Robin Worlie
Roxanne Gates
Samantha Wright
Sandra McClure
Sarah Hackel
Sarah Leigh Bissette
Sarah Tesch
Shana Short
Sharon Snyder
Stacie Moody
Sue Fleming
Susan McMahan
Susie Oldaker
Tammy McKinney
Taytum Rucker
Teri Alcaraz
Tina Bland
Tori McFadden
Tracy Baugh
Tracy Britton
Tracy Timm
Trish Vandenbosch
Vanessa Speigle
Veronica Verastique
Vicki Baumer
Vicky Epps
Victoria (Vicki) Kron

INDEX

The material in this book is for informational purposes only and is not intended as a substitute for the advice and care of your physician. As with all new diet and nutrition regimens, the program described in this book should be followed only after first consulting with your physician to make sure it is appropriate to your individual circumstances. The author and publisher expressly disclaim responsibility for any adverse effects that may result fro the use or application of the information contained in this book.

Copyright © 2021 by Maya Krampf

All rights reserved.
Published in the United States by MPK Publishing
www.wholesomeyum.com
Wholesome Yum is a registered trademark.

Library of Congress Cataloging-in-Publication Data is available upon request.

ISBN: 978-1-7370131-0-5
Ebook: 978-1-7370131-1-2

Printed in China

Book cover and interior design by LeAnna Weller Smith
Photographs by Maya Krampf
Author photograph by Oleg Krampf
Photo editing by Lesley Dykes

10 9 8 7 6 5 4 3 2 1

First Edition